Ministry Makeover

Ministry Makeover
Recovering a Theology for Bi-vocational Service in the Church

BY
ROSARIO PICARDO

FOREWORD BY
MIKE SLAUGHTER

WIPF & STOCK · Eugene, Oregon

MINISTRY MAKEOVER
Recovering a Theology for Bi-vocational Service in the Church

Copyright © 2015 Rosario Picardo. All rights reserved. Except for brief quotations in critical publications or reviews, no part of this book may be reproduced in any manner without prior written permission from the publisher. Write: Permissions. Wipf and Stock Publishers, 199 W. 8th Ave., Suite 3, Eugene, OR 97401.

Wipf & Stock
An Imprint of Wipf and Stock Publishers
199 W. 8th Ave., Suite 3
Eugene, OR 97401

www.wipfandstock.com

ISBN 13: 978-1-62564-650-7

Manufactured in the U.S.A.   02/05/2015

Contents

Foreword by Mike Slaughter | vii

1 An Alarming Decline | 1
2 Bright Spots of Hope | 7
3 Rethinking Resources | 15
4 Biblical Precedents for Bi-vocational Ministry | 23
5 Lessons from Early Revivalists | 46
6 A Theology of Work for the Church | 61
7 A Bi-vocational Prognosis | 65
8 Rethinking Church | 87

Bibliography | 91

Foreword

IF THERE WERE EVER an era in the history of the church where new wine needed to be poured into new wineskins, we are living it today. And young, passionate pastors like Rosario (Roz) Picardo are just the ones to lead the pouring. As Roz points out in *Ministry Makeover: Recovering a Theology for Bi-vocational Service in the Church*, the mainline church within the United States has been in a serious decline over the past forty years. Attendance, professions of faith, participation by the age twenty-one and under demographic, and the very number of churches themselves have dramatically decreased. In *Ministry Makeover*, Rosario explores the underlying causes for these discouraging statistics, numbers that represent real lives and kingdom opportunities lost, and then builds a compelling case as to why embracing bi-vocational and incarnational missionary methods to implement new congregations is the most viable way forward for reaching the least and the lost in a post-Christendom world.

Rosario is not only the "preacher" for these concepts, he is an experienced practitioner. In 2008 as a "parachute drop" pastor, he moved into a challenging urban neighborhood in Lexington, Kentucky, with no staff, no building, and very little funding to found Embrace Church, now a multisite movement that is attracting and serving diverse communities across three campuses. Necessity is the mother of invention, and Rosario found himself in the perfect living laboratory for identifying effective ways of reaching neighbors for Christ and then launching them into their own kingdom callings.

Although I had been aware of Rosario's ministry for quite some time, it was just recently that I was privileged to have Roz join the staff team at Ginghamsburg Church, the large United Methodist congregation I pastor just north of Dayton, Ohio. Our vision is to plant or revitalize one thousand new churches by 2050. As the Executive Pastor of New Church Development, Rosario will lead and accomplish this vision by continuing to dream and deploy the approaches posited in this book.

Rosario is both a dreamer and a doer, and I am excited about what God has planned ahead for the Ginghamsburg missional movement through his leadership.

Mike Slaughter
Lead Pastor
Ginghamsburg Church

1

An Alarming Decline

SINCE THE MERGER OF 1968, the United Methodist Church has declined every year. It has gained some attention, but not as much as the dwindling financial resources. It is hard to conceive the financial problem when net assets have increased by 217 percent to total over $52 billion dollars. Total giving has increased by 144 percent, and total giving by worshipers has increased by 178 percent. These totals take into account the inflation rate as of 2009. The finances, without a doubt, have increased at a significant rate since 1968, but the expenses have unfortunately grown at the even more alarming rate of 44 percent after inflation.[1]

The real financial problem is, as Lovett H. Weems says, that "virtually everything related to people went down, such as the number of churches, worship attendance, membership, professions of faith, and children and youth."[2] While the spending has gone up, the giving has gone down, and that was exacerbated by the 2008 recession, where there was a $60 million dollar decline.[3] With no new people coming in, and the main givers in the UMC aging, it is the same people carrying a heavier load, and it is crushing them. For instance, more than 10,000 of our 35,000 local churches have thirty-five or fewer people present for worship on a typical

---

1. Weems, *Focus*, 212.
2. Ibid., 219.
3. Ibid., 235.

Sunday. The vast majority of these churches were built to serve the population as it was one hundred years ago, when 40 percent of Americans made their living by farming.[4] This is a clear indication that people are leaving the church, and it is time for pastors and congregations to work on addressing why this is happening.

There are practical solutions to make a stopgap financially, but that does not necessarily solve the problems related to vision/mission, attracting new people, and creating vitality in the life of a congregation. Not to say that the following are not important, but instead of focusing on spending cuts, reducing the sizes of districts and annual conferences, and creating programs, there has to be more of a focus on building people up, and the greatest avenue to do this is in the local church. This calls for investing in the major players, who are the clergy and laity. This also calls for focus on the gap that exists between these two parties.

In order to understand the current reality of the United Methodist Church (UMC) and mainline denominations, the first priority is to understand and define the problem. Christendom in the United States is no longer a cultural norm, and mainline denominations have been directly affected by this reality. The fact remains that since the 1968 merger in Dallas between the Methodists and Evangelical United Brethren, the newly formed UMC has experienced decline in North America for over forty years. The decline was even taking place for both denominations prior to the merger. Extensive research shows that by 1970 the UMC reported a total membership of 10,671,744 and 40,653 organized churches. In a fourteen-year period, by 1984 the UMC had lost 13 percent of its total membership, bringing it down to 9,266,853. That translates to a weekly loss of 1,930 members. Worship attendance declined by 11 percent in that fourteen-year period, and 2,665 local churches closed their doors. The UMC is not the only mainline denomination that declined in total membership and worship attendance, resulting in church closures. The Episcopal Church, the United Church of Christ, the Christian Church (Disciples of Christ), Presbyterian Church in America (PCA), and the

---

4. Rendle, *Journey in the Wilderness*, 3127.

Presbyterian Church in the United States of America (PCUSA) all saw this same trend.[5]

Recent studies by experts such as Lovett Weems through the Lewis Leadership Center show how numbers have continued to decline when it comes to virtually every category involving people. Weems shows this in figure 1 to illustrate the point.[6]

FIGURE 1.

The Decline

Decreases: 2009 as % of 1968

Number of churches: 80%

Worship attendance: 78%

Membership: 71%

Professions of faith: 57%

Children and youth:* 44%

---

*Children and youth figures begin with 1974 when they were reported for the first time.

The previous statistics show how decline has hampered the UMC; however, it is important to note increases that have taken place since the 1960s. Such increases have been in categories like net assets, with growth through endowments, buildings, and property. Also, total giving and spending per giving unit have increased because of inflation. Figure 2 shows how dramatically statistics involving money have increased over time since the 1968 merger.[7]

---

5. Willimon and Wilson, "Rekindling the Flame."
6. Weems, *Focus*, 223.
7. Ibid., 207-11.

FIGURE 2.

Giving and Assets

Increases: 2009 as % of 1968

Net Assets: 217%

Total giving: 144%

Giving per worshiper: 178%

The 1968 figures are adjusted for inflation to 2009 dollars.

Nearly 28,000 UMC churches reported having no building debt in 2009 but had appreciated building assets including parsonages that totaled over $52 billion. Churches have spent a lot more. After taking inflation into account, the difference translates into a 44 percent spending increase. Because of discipleship and other church programs, people are giving more to the mission of the UMC, but the churches are drawing from a smaller membership base, and a majority of givers are over the age of seventy years old.[8]

Unfortunately this all began to change in 2008 with the economic meltdown and the housing crisis. The United States entered the worst recession since the Great Depression. The following statistics reveal the severity of the recession:

- At least 8 million jobs were lost, with 740,000 jobs lost in January 2009 alone.
- Americans lost $13 trillion in wealth.
- Hundreds of bank failures.
- The S&P 500 dropped 57 percent from its high in 2007 with an almost stock market panic mentality.
- In some parts of the country, home prices fell 32 percent.
- According to RealityTrac Inc, the Great Recession caused 2.5 million homes to be foreclosed on, with millions more having

---
8. Ibid., 219.

foreclosure filings, and by 2009, one in forty-five homes were in default.

- By March 2009, Citigroup stock was worth $1 per share and Bank of America was at $3 per share.[9]

The recession of 2008 impacted most nonprofits, churches, and denominations, including the UMC. In 2009 the UMC did not recover financially, with a decline of $60 million.[10] When the UMC was growing, as most mainline denominations were in the 1950s, the average age was younger than the rest of the general population. Today, the UMC is aging, and in 2009, the death rate had increased 35 percent since the UMC's inception in 1968.[11]

The declining people numbers of attendance, membership, and professions of faith, and the increased prices from inflation and average age of members all culminate to what Lovett Weems, UMC expert and director of the Lewis Center for Church Leadership at Wesley Theological Seminary, calls the *Death Tsunami*.[12] One reason for Weems's rationale is the likelihood that between 2021 and 2050 there will be an increase in death rate that has not been seen since the 1940s. There will be more deaths in 2050 than in 2010 by 50 percent.[13] The preoccupation for local churches to make budget every year with dwindling attendance interferes with the mission of "making disciples of Jesus Christ for the transformation of the world."[14] Weems believes that this could be an opportunity for the UMC, jurisdictions, annual conferences, districts, and local churches, to reset a financial baseline and focus on mission and outreach. This has already taken place with the 2016 general conference lowering the number of delegates to save money and a number of annual conferences shortening their days

9. Montana, "What Caused?"
10. Ibid., 237.
11. Ibid., 256.
12. Ibid., 261.
13. Ibid., 273.
14. "Mission Statement," in *Book of Discipline*, 87.

to cut budgets for both conferences and local churches that send pastors and delegates.[15]

All of these declining statistics can be depressing. The worship attendance, lay participation, and budgets are down, but does that mean it's too late for the church to experience renewal? I believe God's work is not finished, and perhaps God desires to do a new thing with new wineskins.

As an urban church planter that ministers to people on the margins, funding was a hard thing to come by. Restarting a dying urban church with a decaying building and starting two more communities inside of my church plant called Embrace Church in Lexington, Kentucky, about killed me. I never would have dreamed Embrace Church would become a movement with a total of four communities. There was no way I could keep up with this organic movement of God without some help. The problem was I did not have the type of budget that would allow me to hire staff, so I needed God to give me a new wineskin. That new wineskin came in the form of bi-vocational pastors and urban missionaries.

---

15. Ibid., 373.

2

Bright Spots of Hope

MANY MAINLINE DENOMINATIONS AND church planting networks understand that one of the most effective ways to reach people for Christ is by planting new Christian faith communities. The wisest initiative the UMC has implemented over the last quadrennium is the Path 1 initiative to plant 650 congregations. Although they fell short of the goal, they still planted 621 churches, which provided an overall growth of 223 percent since the 2004-2007 quadrennium. The UMC reports they are planting at a rate of "11.5 new church[es] per month (compared with 4.23 new church starts per month from 2004-2007)."[1] Since the success of the Path 1 initiative, they have set the audacious goal of planting 1,000 new congregations by the end of the 2013-2016 quadrennium.[2] The breakdown in figure 3 shows that the majority of the faith communities that were planted were in the South Eastern Jurisdiction (SEJ).

1. Shockley, "New Church Starts Update," 1.
2. Ibid.

FIGURE 3.

Jurisdictional Snapshot of Church Planting Activity[3]

	NCJ	NEJ	SCJ	SEJ	WJ	Total
2008	20	12	31	53	12	128
2009	35	17	30	38	25	145
2010	38	20	37	55	15	165
2011	31	25	22	50	8	136
2012	24	18	26	36	6	110
Total	148	92	146	232	66	684

The congregations represented many different types of models in church planting, such as: conference starts (an annual conference decides to plant a faith community in a geographical area where no UMC churches exist); connectional "parachute drop" projects (a planter is appointed to a certain area without existing relationships, launch team, or facility to start); partner church projects (a healthy church gives birth to a new church start in a mother-daughter scenario or multiple churches support one new church start); multisite projects (a congregation attempts to multiply itself in other geographical areas and venues); Elijah/Elisha projects (a new church start is birthed out of a dying congregation or one tries to "pass the mantle"); vital mergers (two or more declining/dying churches coming together under a new vision to become a church plant); church-within-a-church (an existing congregation attempts to reach a different demographic within their community in a second service); nontraditional (missional or monastic communities that are more grassroots but still seek to multiply themselves); surprise birth projects (a church from another denomination may choose to affiliate with the UMC or a ministry may seek to become a church); lay-led projects (laity who may not

---

3. Ibid. This figure is adapted from the report giving by Gary Shockley to convey the breakdown of where churches have been planted within the UMC in the United States.

have the credentials nor education plant a new faith community); part-time projects (bi-vocational or part-time pastors plant who are working a job as tentmakers); and racial-ethnic projects (multiethnic church plants trying to reach groups outside of the traditional Anglo-Saxon UMC churches that are in existence).[4]

All of the above models mentioned abide to certain characteristics that Path 1 defines as a faith community. The characteristics are:

- Theologically Wesleyan
- Worship frequently and celebrate the sacraments
- Have effective systems for developing disciples of Jesus Christ
- Teach and practice biblical stewardship
- Are missional and work toward community transformation
- Receive new members
- Will embed multiplying DNA in all ministries and plant other new congregations in 3-5 years
- Will remain connected and accountable to the United Methodist Church[5]

Though the strategies may vary, the characteristics of planting congregations according to Path 1 should share similarities in DNA while the methodology varies extensively based on approach, planter, and context.

While the UMC is declining in America, there have been bright spots because of Path 1. For instance, in 2011 the two annual conferences that grew the most, while the rest either declined or plateaued, were the Kentucky and the Greater New Jersey Conferences. The Kentucky Conference planted fifteen churches in the last quadrennium, which led to overall membership and attendance growth. It was the largest growth they had seen in nearly

---

4. Ibid.
5. "Characteristics of New Church Starts," http://www.path1.org/characteristics.php.

sixteen years. A focus on planting new churches leads to growth.[6] Also, the Greater New Jersey Conference witnessed growth in membership and attendance for the first time in forty-five years. It is because both of these annual conferences prioritized church planting instead of focusing on revitalization.[7]

If church planting is so critical to growth in reaching the lost and in reinvigorating the institution to become a movement again, then it needs to be prioritized accordingly. Perhaps the sale of empty buildings and the liquidation of assets from dying congregations can be the seed where new life is found. After all, Jesus put it best when he told his disciples preceding his death, "I tell you the truth, unless a kernel of wheat is planted in the soil and dies, it remains alone. But its death will produce many new kernels—a plentiful harvest of new lives."[8] Also, the reduction of apportionment dollars in order to invest that money back into local churches can transform the UMC from the bottom all the way to the top; this will be more effective than relying on a "top-down" approach. The possibilities of how many churches can be planted could be endless with more resources being redirected into movements such as church planting, instead of preserving the institution where the upper echelon receives pay increases and more general agencies are created.

Desperation and decline often lead to innovation, as seen with Path 1. This has opened up major opportunities for church planters and clergy, but there is another initiative that has been created by Path 1 that leads right to the roots of early Methodism and the early church. It has to do with laity taking on more of a role as bi-vocational leaders. This has been labeled as the Lay Missionary Planting Network (LMPN). The LMPN tagline is fitting: "Equipping Ordinary People for an Extraordinary Harvest."[9] It is founded on Acts 4:13 which states, "Now when they saw the

---

6. Hahn, "2011 Numbers."

7. Ibid.

8. John 12:24 ESV. Unless otherwise noted, all Scripture references are taken from the ESV.

9. "Lay Missionary Planting Network Training," http://path1.org/lmpn.

boldness of Peter and John, and perceived that they were uneducated, common men, they were astonished. And they recognized that they had been with Jesus." The LMPN vision to reach the harvest is as follows:

> We believe that all persons, whether clergy or laity, have been called by God for specific ministries, for which we want to prepare them. The network training experience should help clarify the learner's sense of call and solidify the person's commitment to church planting. The ultimate goal of the curriculum: to equip laypersons with the knowledge, skills, and abilities to be United Methodist church planters.[10]

The curriculum is done in ten sessions to equip laity in the basics of church planting, scripture, doctrine, and Wesleyan theology. The hope is to deploy people and teams as needed when a new church is ready to form. Also, the curriculum is translated into Spanish and is soon to be translated into other languages as well. As the United States enters another time of "golden immigration," reaching out to a diversity of ethnic groups presents enormous opportunities. As mentioned previously, the growth of both the Kentucky Annual Conference and the Greater New Jersey Conference was a direct result of church planting. However, the communities that were targeted were not only Anglos, but also growing immigrant communities such as Haitians, Brazilians, Hispanics, Korean Americans, and people from various African countries. The LMPN would allow people to serve in a bi-vocational capacity who may not have a seminary degree, let alone a college or high school diploma, to be engaged in significant kingdom work.[11] This is reminiscent of early Methodism, as George Hunter points out,

> Eighteenth-century Methodists were an entrepreneurial laity; lay people invented many ministries to serve people in their community. In some communities, lay Methodists gathered children to give them the only organized education they might ever experience. Lay people started

10. Ibid.
11. Ibid.

most of the new classes and societies. Lay people brought Methodist Christianity across the Atlantic. And when they wrote to Wesley, "Send some preachers to help us," they did not ask Wesley, "Send some preachers to do all the ministry for us!"[12]

This not only sounds like early Methodism but even more so like early Christianity. In this day and age, people who are called into vocational ministry cannot afford to take out a significant amount of debt to go to college or receive a seminary degree.

The LMPN is paving the way for glimpses of a promising future for the UMC, despite the denomination's overall decline. Lay people will have a bigger role to play in leading churches, especially if/when the financial tsunami plays out, and churches will not be able to afford to pay ordained elders their increasing equitable compensations along with providing benefits that include skyrocketing insurance costs, housing allowances, pensions, and other investments. The UMC must return to a movement, as Bruce Larson points out where the laity is more entrusted with the ministry as it is in other parts of the world where the church is actually growing such as in China.[13]

Many of the budgetary cuts that happen are for the UMC church to live within its financial means and to experience longer-term sustainability. The temptation is to settle for a survival-mode mentality instead of a thriving-church mentality. Weems suggests that this financial baseline reset could be an opportunity for a new and focused vitality. Weems proposes to start with reallocating funds for new church development. Annual conference needs to reallocate funds from programs that are ineffective and not working to the future of the church. With all of the assets many annual conferences have, it would be beneficial for them to liquidize some of them by selling off the facilities of churches that have closed in order to use those funds for a new work or restarting churches. An example of this type of work is happening in the Virginia Annual Conference. They call it the *Elijah Church*. The Elijah Church

12. Hunter, *Recovery*, 297-300.
13. Ibid., 321.

is helping to renew struggling congregations who are desperate enough to make a change in outreach and effectiveness. After the church and conference agree to a need for change, they together begin to explore options such as:

1. A renewed vision for revitalization,
2. Relocation,
3. Merger with another church and relocation to a new site, and
4. Merger with another congregation using one of the current facilities[14]

Elijah churches take everything they have to invest in something new by giving the biblical example of Elijah giving Elisha a double portion of his spirit by passing on the mantle. The Elijah churches are recognized and celebrated at the Virginia Annual Conference for their past efforts and willingness to invest in the future by either:

1. Continuing while permitting a new ministry to begin in their building,
2. Joining another church and giving the building to reach new populations, or
3. Joining another church and investing the church assets in new churches.[15]

Elijah church is simply one of many ways to let a dying congregation pass away in a dignifying way while birthing life to something new. This is an example many Annual Conferences throughout Methodism can emulate.

Weems has another method to reset the financial baseline of the UMC. It has to do with eliminating the equitable salary and having no minimum salary. This is in part due to the fact that a majority of UMC churches are being served by part-time and licensed local pastors because the number of local churches that

---

14. Ibid., 455.
15. Ibid., 458.

can support the salary package of an ordained elder or deacon is diminishing rapidly. In the future, if equitable salaries and minimum salaries are not eliminated or lowered it could prove to be catastrophic across the board for the UMC.[16] As many annual conferences are making tough decisions to do ministry within their financial means, Kentucky is lowering its budget for the first time in its history. Bishop Lindsey Davis said, "Across our Annual Conference we have experienced over $300,000 in salary reduction as a result of congregations reducing salary support to our clergy. This fact alone makes it inevitable that many of our pastors will move at a salary decrease. While these reductions are not fair to our clergy they are part of our current reality."[17] A South Eastern Jurisdictional Annual Conference has never experienced such a reduction; however, this has been the norm in the Northern part of the country for such annual conferences as the New England Annual Conference where a majority of pastors, even ordained, serve multiple charges. Its largest UMC congregation spanning five states only has 150 in worship attendance on a Sunday morning.[18]

The time is approaching that laity are going to have to take a more active role in ministry because religious paid professionals are not going to be as prevalent over the next fifty years, especially in mainline denominations. Also, laity who are feeling a compelling call to vocational ministry are not going to want to be weighed down under $100,000 worth of theological education debt. This is not fair to them or their families. I believe the answer is in deploying bi-vocational pastors and missionaries who can be "tentmakers," and have honest interactions with the folks outside of the established church.

---

16. Ibid., 501.
17. Davis, "2014 Appointments," e-mail to author, April 10, 2014.
18. McKinley, "New England Annual Conference."

3

Rethinking Resources

CHURCH PLANTING IS A significant way for the church to rethink resources. Asbury Theological Seminary has even taken the role of church planting to the next level by instituting a master of arts in church planting through a $5-million gift that was given to initiate it. The gift was given to follow Asbury's 2023 Strategic Plan that anticipates 40 percent of the graduates will participate in church planting.[1] The church planting program will provide a 100 percent tuition scholarship to those selected. Asbury describes the need for a focus on church planting by stating,

> New churches are a vital evangelism tool. As the global church continues to grow, there is a desperate need for trained church planters with skills in personal evangelism, leadership, and organizational theory. Churches still need to be planted in North America, and because of the changing demographics of communities, church planting has become a cross-cultural task. The Master of Arts in Church Planting will train students in the theological, theoretical, and practical literatures of church planting. Students will receive practical experience in planting churches through experiential learning, and will learn the art of intercultural understanding and

---

1. "Asbury Seminary Receives Commitment," AsburySeminary.edu, http://asburyseminary.edu/kentucky/asbury-seminary-receives-commitment-5-million-gift-launch-church-planting-initiative.

contextualization. Students who complete this course of study will be equipped to plant churches in various cultures to which God calls them.[2]

The notion that "new churches are a vital evangelism tool" is essential in understanding why church planting is so important. Based on the blatant decline in many mainline denominations, it is evident that existing churches are struggling to maintain a position of relevance and witness within society. As a result, many churches are not able to engage in evangelism effectively, which is at the heart of the role of the church. Evangelism comes from the Koine Greek word "euangelion," which simply means "to proclaim the gospel or good news." It is the role of the church to share and expose people to the good news of Jesus Christ's birth, life, crucifixion, resurrection and ascension. Then, it is through evangelism that people feel drawn to God, connect with the church, and hopefully grow to become devoted followers of Christ. Since a number of existing churches have become ineffective in reaching people, new churches are able to break free from the characteristics of existing churches that have lost people. However, starting a new faith community is no easy task. It requires not only certain spiritual graces, but also natural skill and knowledge. This is why Asbury Seminary's investment in a full course of study in church planting and graduate student scholarships in this area is so important.

Another way for the church to rethink its resources is rooted in the role of bi-vocational ministers and ordained elders adopting John Perkins's Christian Community Development Association (CCDA) model. He asserts that if clergy can be rooted for a significant amount of time in a given geographical area, the relationship between the clergy and church would be strengthened, as would be the church's relationship with the community. Perkins has three rules for a significant ministry to take place, which he calls the "Three Rs." They are relocation, reconciliation, and redistribution.[3]

---

2. "M.A. in Church Planting," Asbury Theological Seminary, http://asburyseminary.edu/academics/degrees/master-of-arts/m-a-in-church-planting.

3. Perkins, *With Justice for All*, 118.

First, Perkins argues that to effectively minister to the poor one must relocate into their neighborhoods. The same is true for those clergy who want to reach a given geographical area or target focus for their local churches. They can relocate into a specific neighborhood of people they want to reach, get to know the people, and build relationships. This process can take years, but the potential results are well worth the effort. Essentially, relocation is incarnational ministry at its core. As Perkins points out, "This is why relocation, the first of the three Rs, is so important. An outsider can seldom know the needs of the community well enough to know how to best respond to them. Rarely if ever can an outsider effectively lead the community in finding creative solutions to its own problems. That kind of leadership, the kind of leadership that empowers people, comes from insiders."[4] Perkins believes relocation at its best is done when one becomes an insider in a community instead of an outsider trying to respond to the given needs of a community. Insiders are people who can empower others.[5] Relocation is essential to make a lasting impact on a community and understand its assets, potential, and problems.

The key with relocation is relationship building. Something really special happens when people spend meaningful time together. When a person takes the time to get to know someone and especially those on the margins, s/he becomes less judgmental and more open to their story and their struggle. When leaders become neighbors, this goes a step further, and in a way, their stories become intertwined; their struggle becomes interconnected. This makes a huge difference because it seems so easy to dismiss other people and the intimate details of what goes on in the community. When someone commits to the neighborhood where s/he serves, s/he becomes a member of the community so that whatever happens there becomes a joint issue and concern. Likewise, the leader is able to share personally in the work and joys of seeing transformation occur in the community. Now, there are people who are gifted to serve a community wholeheartedly without having

4. Ibid., 654.
5. Ibid.

to relocate per se. However, these individuals tend to fall into the minority and not the majority of those engaged in the missional work of ministry.

Essentially, relocation is incarnational ministry at its core. The Christian story begins with God relocating from heaven to earth in the person of Jesus Christ in order to do life with humanity. The Gospel of John 1:1–5 and 14 records:

> In the beginning was the Word, and the Word was with God, and the Word was God. He was in the beginning with God. All things were made through him, and without him was not any thing made that was made. In him was life, and the life was the light of men. The light shines in the darkness, and the darkness has not overcome it . . . And the Word became flesh and dwelt among us, and we have seen his glory, glory as of the only Son from the Father, full of grace and truth.

The holy mystery of how God becomes flesh through the second person of the Trinity and dwells among us, or becomes our neighbor, is one of the most significant components of the Christian faith. It sends the message to humanity that location and getting to know people intimately are both very important to God. There is something profound in the simplicity of being present and being willing to experience life with others. Jesus did not have to live with humanity, especially not as a modest carpenter's son, but he chose to do so. Jesus's example is one of placing others at the center instead of the self, one that embraces people, as is evidenced by his relationship with the disciples and countless others throughout the Scripture. Clearly, God is concerned about relationships, and relocating is one way for leaders to show that s/he is concerned, too.

Relocation can be lived out through bi-vocational ministry as a person becomes one with the community and his or her work environment. Often times it is easy for pastors to become isolated from the "real world" because they do not get the type of interactions with unchurched folks as they would in a normal work setting. Relocation for a bi-vocational pastor would require building relationships with co-workers in meaningful ways that could open doors for conversation about faith.

The second R is reconciliation. All Christians are called to be bridges in reconciling unbelievers and apostates to God. Specifically, it is imperative for clergy not just to relocate into a given neighborhood or area, but to move into significant relationships with the hope of engaging others in the ministry of reconciliation. The ministry of reconciling, or bringing together again, implies that restoration is required where something has been broken or pushed apart. In Christianity, sin has "broken apart" humanity's relationship with God. This is an alienation suffered by all since Romans 3:23 explains that no one is exempt from sinning and falling short of God's glory. However, there is good news for those who believe in Jesus Christ. The Apostle Paul declares in 2 Corinthians 5:18-20,

> All this is from God, who through Christ reconciled us to himself and gave us the ministry of reconciliation; that is, in Christ God was reconciling the world to himself, not counting their trespasses against them, and entrusting to us the message of reconciliation. Therefore, we are ambassadors for Christ, God making his appeal through us. We implore you on behalf of Christ, be reconciled to God.[6]

Through Jesus the world has been reconciled to God. The relationship between God and humanity has been mended. Because of the work of the Savior, people no longer need a mediator in order to approach God but can go boldly to the throne of grace (Heb 4:16). Although, this seems like a simple concept, it is difficult for most people to grasp. The idea that what we do wrong will not be held against us because of Christ seems too good to be true. So, it takes a renewing of the mind (Rom 12:2) for people to really get it and experience the transformation that is referenced in the same verse of Romans.

With respect to resources, traditionally, the church is understood to be the primary venue and expression of faith where

---

6. This is a pivotal verse used for reconciliation between God and humanity.

people encounter this biblical reality of reconciliation for those who become connected to Christ. So, if there is a decline in mainstream denominations, there has to be a decline in the ministry of reconciliation, which will have an adverse effect on the influence of the proclamation of the gospel. Another dynamic to this reconciliation is not only the forging of an intimate relationship between God and humanity, but also within humanity. In turn, the church will continue to suffer based on the current trajectory of decline in certain mainstream denominations, if something is not done to reverse this pattern. It is within reason to assert that of the existing churches experiencing decline, some of them can be revitalized and infused with new life if given the right leadership team and proper resources. However, there are some churches that are dead and should close. Even though this may seem like a harsh assessment, it is true, and it is time for the governing bodies to acknowledge this reality more. The planting of new churches then becomes a solution to help infuse new life back into situations where there was once spiritual death and decline.

The third R is redistribution. Redistribution is a tangible way of loving one's neighbor as oneself. This involves sacrifice, maybe it even means being willing to live less comfortably, and placing ministry ahead of having a large a salary. As Perkins believes, redistribution is sharing more and committing to empower people who are living on the margins in a community.[7] Perkins argues, "As a first step toward redistribution, we must commit ourselves to living with less in order that we can share more. This process of finding ways to use less can be a lifelong family adventure. Yet living more simply will not in itself make much difference in the lives of the poor. We must find ways to use what we save to empower the needy."[8] Jesus said the poor would always be in our midst. The reality is, poverty is not just a lack of financial resources, but also the lack of godly relationships to help connect others to the reconciling power of Christ's love. Everybody is powerless without God. Redistribution is practicing holiness in a social context.

7. Hunter, *Recovery*, 1710.
8. Ibid.

Rethinking Resources

Perkins's understanding of redistribution is powerful on a personal level and a corporate level. From a personal perspective, the idea of growing as a family to the point of living off of minimal resources so that more can be given for the uplift of the community as a whole is transformational. As Jesus points out, we will always have the poor with us, which may seem overwhelming at first. The physical needs alone of the impoverished members in the community are tremendous. However, through Jesus's example, his ministry of feeding the hungry, his encouragement to the disciples to live simple lives of minimal materialism, and numerous scriptures commanding believers to care for the poor, it is clear that Christians are called to help meet these needs. Consequently, if families collectively make it a practice to live off of less and share with others out of what becomes their excess, the needs of the impoverished will continuously decrease. This sense of caring for one another in community is seen throughout the Bible, and further supports the impact that personal redistribution can have on transformative community engagement.

From a corporate perspective, if the church should practice this same principle of redistribution, then there would be a shift in the entire financial structure of most churches. For a start, churches with the most resources would no longer spend an exorbitant amount of money on multimillion-dollar facilities and expensive furnishings that are mostly for show. Pastors in the top tier of the salary bracket would no longer receive a six-figure income and allowances for excessive material possessions. By starting with just these two areas alone, millions of dollars in kingdom resources would become available. These funds would be redirected into building up people, the community, and the intangible spread God's kingdom. From here, churches on every level would evaluate how funds are being stewarded, make nonessential cuts, and redistribute their resources of people, services, and finances in the areas that will yield the greatest impact for God's kingdom.

Within the UMC, the increase in expenses and long-lasting decline in attendance, membership, professions of faith, baptisms, and younger people have created desperation for revival and renewal. In particular, the United Methodist Church can once again return to being a grassroots movement, by investing more in clergy and laity with the common mission "to make disciples of Jesus Christ for the transformation of the world."[9] However, this investment is not one that should be made in terms of increased compensation for clergy. Instead, clergy and laity would be encouraged and challenged to grow in their understanding of the *priesthood of all believers* through a Trinitarian lens. They would also be challenged to rethink resources and consider the bi-vocational model as a viable ministry option. Ultimately, there is a hunger to once again thrive in a new way by starting a new work. The harvest is the largest it has ever been in the United States, making it the third largest mission field in the world. There is an opportunity to reach the nearly 200 million unchurched people in the United States. However, the UMC must redefine the relationship between clergy, laity, and the governing denominational bodies, and also redefine what it means to do ministry in a changing culture.[10] As a part of this redefinition, the UMC will benefit greatly by embracing this principle of corporate redistribution and leading the movement for other suffering denominations and churches in general to follow.

---

9. "Mission Statement," in *Book of Discipline*, 87.
10. Hunter, *Recovery*, 489.

4

Biblical Precedents for Bi-vocational Ministry

THROUGHOUT SCRIPTURE, THERE SEEMS to be precedence for bi-vocational ministry. Three of many scriptural examples will be examined here. The Old Testament figures that will be examined are the prophet Amos and Nehemiah, and the New Testament figure is the Apostle Paul. My intent is to first explore the social context in which they lived and how God used them through their specialized bi-vocational ministries.

AMOS

For one to understand Amos, the man and the prophet, one must understand the complexity of the historical context and setting of Israel in the eighth century BC. The historical markers of Amos's prophetic ministry were between the reigns of Judah's King Uzziah (783-742 BC) and Israel's King Jeroboam (786–746 BC). Amos 1:1 indicates that Amos came on the scene "two years before the earthquake" that caused great desolation. Unlike Jeremiah and Hosea's prophetic ministries that extended over decades, Amos's lasted only a few months. In addition to a short tenure, Amos had the challenge of traveling outside his comfort zone as a citizen of the southern kingdom of Judah to Israel, the northern kingdom.

He spoke out against the coveted calf idols the Israelites were worshipping at Gilgal, Dan, and Bethel. Like the prophets of old, Amos found himself calling Israel back to honor the covenant they made with Yahweh and to repentance. At the point of Amos's prophetic tenure, Israel had backslidden into idolatry, sexual immorality, and oppressing those in poverty.[1]

There is a uniqueness found in Amos that sets him apart from his prophetic predecessors. It is not the fiery prophetic message that echoes some of the postexilic prophets, but instead he is distinguished by how he characterized himself. At the start of his writing, he identifies himself as, according to Amos 1:1, "among the shepherds of Tekoa." As a shepherd, and/or herdsman, Amos would have been on the low end of the social totem pole. During the eighth century BC, shepherds were in the lower echelons of society, and often despised. Amos would have simply been viewed as an uneducated, illiterate, blue-collar farmhand.[2] Amos 7:14-15 further drives this point: "I was no prophet, nor a prophet's son, but I was a herdsman and a dresser of sycamore figs. But the Lord took me from following the flock, and the Lord said to me, 'Go, prophesy to my people Israel.'"[3]

A pertinent question would then be how did Amos support himself while living in a foreign land in order that he might deliver his radical message? The scholar Daniel Hays suggests that Amos was not just a simple sheepherder, but rather that he owned an extensive flock that helped support his ministry.[4] It is impossible to determine whether Amos had wealth, and quite frankly wealth is irrelevant to this issue. Through his vocation as a sheepherder, Amos is used by God to identify with the oppressed and to speak against their oppressors. Amos spoke on behalf of people who were being oppressed economically.[5]

---

1. Hays and Longman, "Overview of Amos," 4347-57.
2. Blanchard, "Amos."
3. Amos 7:14-15.
4. Ibid., 4384-90.
5. Giles, "Note on the Vocation of Amos."

Amos was not demeaning his own prophetic calling when he explained to the priest Amaziah that he was "not a prophet, or . . . the son of a prophet." On the contrary, he was affirming it, for he did not ask for it, but it was Yahweh that took him from his flock. Amos looked at himself in a humble way, as a simple herdsman and fig farmer who performed in a blue-collar occupation, not as a prophet dependent on a prophetic organization where he received mentoring from an elder prophet. Instead, he set himself apart from the comfort of any organized guild of prophets. The fact that Amos earned his own livelihood as a herdsmen and fig farmer afforded him the advantage of speaking the words Yahweh put in his mouth, instead of giving in to the pressures of fearing those he would offend. As the scholar Fred Wood puts it, Amos was giving his "declaration of independence," in which he spoke boldly against the injustices of his day.[6]

The fact that Amos's occupation is disclosed separates him from the Old Testament's sixteen writing prophets. Amos is only concerned about the burning message given to him from Yahweh, and is less concerned about the manner in which it is received by Amaziah and Israel. Since his sustenance is coming from his occupation, he is not easily persuaded by others and is able to defend his call as a prophet with boldness. Old Testament scholar John Thomas Finley supports the conclusion that Amos was a bi-vocational prophet:

> When Amos goes on to state his occupation, he apparently replies directly to Amaziah's implication that prophecy is the source of his food. In other words, Amos denies that he makes a living from prophecy, or at least that material gain in any way motivates his actions. Right now he is not making his living through the office of a prophet. The contrast can be brought out better, in my view, by the present tense translation: I am not (nor have I ever been) a prophet (by profession).[7]

---

6. Wood, "Clash between Amaziah and Amos," 121.
7. Finley, *Joel, Amos, Obadiah*, 257.

Amos's function as a bi-vocational prophet would have been something foreign to those who were accustomed to the paid religious professionals. In Israel's religious setting, the priests were viewed primarily as tending the shrine at Beth-El. They were adhering to these religious practices and protocols when Amos entered the scene as a type of a lay missionary prophet, who had traveled to a land that was foreign to him. They would have viewed Amos as a lower status laborer with no religious training.[8]

Amaziah was threatened by Amos's prophecy, not only because of his own priestly role, but also because he was trying to protect the interests of King Jeroboam II. Amos's prophecy would have been understood as a form of betrayal and a threat to Israel.[9] In the prior prophetic contexts with which Amaziah was perhaps familiar, a prophet was more than a proclaimer of Yahweh. He or she also functioned in several roles required by the monarchy. For example, 1 Kings 22 states that four hundred prophets advised King Jehoshaphat. It was common for prophets to give guidance on warfare and alliances, as they worked in an advisory role for the king. Also, Amos lacked the type of formal association prophets such as Elijah and Elisha had (2 Kings 2). Amos was a loner who lacked association with any professional guilds, communities, or mentorships.[10]

Amos did not deny being a messenger of Yahweh as much as he denied following the call for self-benefit and the perks that would come from being a prophet in this religious context. Amaziah probably thought that Amos left his small town area in Judah to come to the "big city" in order to make more money as a prophet. Amos may very well have been trying to imply another connection when he said: "But the Lord took me from following the flock, and the Lord said to me, 'Go, prophesy to my people Israel'" (Amos 7:15). This can be seen as a connection to another Old Testament figure that was taken from "the flock" as a shepherd boy, David. Amos was delivering not only the message of Yahweh, but was

8. Ibid.
9. Couey, "Amos," 314.
10. Simundson, Amos and Amaziah.

suggesting that more important than his message was the one who had called him to do it. He was suggesting that God could call the least likely, most unexpected people and use them to transform the culture. Like David, Amos was called to honor Yahweh as King over all of Israel. Amos was called to prophesy to both Israel and Judah, because they were both God's people.[11]

The Greco-Roman philosopher Dio Chrysostom believed that Amos 7:14-15 exhibited Amos's humility in how his calling and prophecy were not something he conjured up on his own or for personal gain. Amos's self-effacing of his prophetic ministry was designed to halt the accusations of Amaziah. Pope Gregory the Great pointed out that as one's service to God increases to a higher level, so should one's level of humility. It was in relation to this that he characterized Amos. Gregory believed it was the work of the Holy Spirit that enabled Amos's humility. The Spirit also called servants like David, Daniel, Peter, Paul, and Matthew from their sole occupational focus to dual roles in serving God with a kingdom-focused vocation. Gregory summarizes it succinctly when he said, "The Spirit changes the human heart in a moment, filling it with light. Suddenly we are no longer what we were; suddenly we are something we never used to be."[12] Even the great reformer John Calvin suggested that Amos was not privileged in the respect that other prophets of old were, because of his lack of any type of prophetic instructional training in the law.[13]

NEHEMIAH

Amos's prophetic call and story are set in the context of humble beginnings as a herdsman and fig farmer. However, it is important to acknowledge that God calls many of the Old Testament figures and prophets from a variety of settings. The story of Nehemiah is one that is set in quite different circumstances than Amos.

---

11. Stuart, *Hosea-Jonah*, 377.
12. Ferreiro and Oden, "Amos 7:1-17," 109-10.
13. Calvin, "Commentary on Amos."

Nehemiah's story opens up in the lavish courts of Persia instead of farm fields.[14] The background leading up to the book of Nehemiah finds Jerusalem in a desolate state as the Babylonian soldiers routed the city, burned the buildings, tore down the temple leaving only the poorest of Jerusalem's people left to pick up the pieces. The Babylonian captivity took the top citizens as deportees to this foreign land, which fulfilled the weeping prophet, Jeremiah's words of destruction. The morale of the people was at an all-time low because of what they witnessed but even more so because they walked in such a long road of disobedience by worshiping false gods and idols while forsaking their first love, Yahweh.[15] After a long seventy years of exile with such prophets as Ezekiel and Daniel bringing a message of hope in a pagan land, the Israelite people bravely returned to their homeland to start over again. As they returned, God raised up prophetic voices along the way to help them trust Yahweh. The voices of Haggai, Zechariah, and Malachi were used to sharpen the people, and their confidence built with each passing day. The rebuilding of the temple was strategized under God's leading by Zerubbabel and Ezra who preached God's Word. Momentum and excitement were building up as God rose up a resourceful leader in Nehemiah to rebuild the broken walls.[16]

Nehemiah's story is set in the mid-fifth century BC where he worked in Susa, the palace of the Persian king Artaxerxes, which ironically was the same setting where the stories of Daniel and Esther took place. Some Old Testament scholars believe the year Nehemiah came on the scene was around 445 BC, which was plausibly thirteen years following Ezra.[17] Old Testament scholar B. W. Anderson believes that Nehemiah's accounts are "one of the most trustworthy sources of Jewish history in the Persian period."[18] The reading of Nehemiah brings an autobiographical sketch that is

---

14. Brown, *Message of Nehemiah*, 13.
15. Ibid.
16. Ibid., 14.
17. Ibid.
18. Anderson, *Living World*, 513.

rarely common in the Old Testament and parallels the accounts in Ezra and Chronicles as well.

Nehemiah is considered one of the great Old Testament figures who displayed extraordinary leadership skills as he led the Israelite people who had been scarred from exile and were uncertain about themselves without a Davidic king. Nehemiah was not a king, prophet, nor priest, but he led in such a manner with characteristics resembling all three roles with his innovation for building projects, repopulating the city, and spiritual reawakening.[19]

Though Old Testament scholars do not view Nehemiah as a prophet in a traditional sense, Nehemiah does function with prophetic qualities when it comes to his calling in Jerusalem (2:12, 17-18), his declaration on behalf of God to the people, his boldness in the face of opposition and oppressiveness (5:13) and his persecution from false prophets (6:10-14). Nehemiah is not priestly like the Levitical priest; however, he participates in spiritual renewal and promotes holiness through prayer, witness, and worship as he leads the people in intercession before God (8:9-12; 9:38-10:1; 12:38). Nehemiah also functions similarly to past Davidic kings such as Hezekiah and Josiah who led religious reforms and building projects/expansions of the temple. God rose Nehemiah up in his time to function in many different roles in order to remind the Israelites of God's love and mercy.[20]

Nehemiah's story is impressive. As a driven, godly leader, it is important to note that in the opening narrative Nehemiah's prime motivation is to be a "servant" of God. The noun "servant" is repeated at the beginning of the memoir in Nehemiah 1:6-11:

> Let your ear be attentive and your eyes open, to hear the prayer of your *servant* that I now pray before you day and night for the people of Israel your servants, confessing the sins of the people of Israel, which we have sinned against you. Even me and my father's house have sinned. We have acted very corruptly against you and have not kept the commandments, the statutes, and the rules

---

19. Brown, *Message of Nehemiah*, 16.
20. Ibid., 17.

that you commanded your servant Moses. Remember the word that you commanded your servant Moses, saying, "If you are unfaithful, I will scatter you among the peoples, but if you return to me and keep my commandments and do them, though your outcasts are in the uttermost parts of heaven, from there I will gather them and bring them to the place that I have chosen, to make my name dwell there." They are your servants and your people, whom you have redeemed by your great power and by your strong hand. O Lord, let your ear be attentive to the prayer of your *servant*, and to the prayer of your servants who delight to fear your name, and give success to your *servant* today, and grant him mercy in the sight of this man.

Nehemiah's highest aspiration is to serve God in whatever capacity necessary. It is important to note that many of the Old Testament figures who are used by God in mighty ways are humble and have an attitude of a servant. After all, this is the *modus operandi* of Jesus Christ, who said in Mark 10:45, "For even the Son of Man came not to be served but to serve, and to give his life as a ransom for many."

Also, it is important to understand that Nehemiah was born in Persia. The tales of Jerusalem being destroyed by the Babylonians were undoubtedly shared with Nehemiah as he was growing up away from the distant land of Jerusalem. In Ezra 4:6-23, there is an understanding that any attempts to rebuild Jerusalem's walls that were in ruins would face major opposition. As a "servant of King Artaxerxes, [Nehemiah is] aware from court news that one innocent attempt to rebuild Jerusalem's walls [has] been dramatically frustrated. At [this] time, local opponents [have] written to the Persian king asserting that Jerusalem's citizens [are] intent on rebellion and, on the king's orders, work on the walls [is] brought to an abrupt end."[21] Even Nehemiah's contemporary Ezra has opposition as the second round of exiles are returning to their homeland.

Nehemiah's deep concern is the exiles returning to their homeland and also rebuilding the walls of Jerusalem. The task in

---

21. Brown, *Message of Nehemiah*, 31.

front of him is challenging and seems impossible to many. Nevertheless, Nehemiah accepts God's call to carry out the task even though his position is cupbearer for King Artaxerxes. Nehemiah functions more as a bi-vocational minister because his "day job" is working for the king, but his call is to rebuild the wall and people.

Nehemiah's day job as a cupbearer for King Artaxerxes is a well-respected position according to a contemporary Greek historian, Herodotus. "The wine steward [is] a man of recognized dignity in court circles, entirely trustworthy, the king's confidant, and next in rank of princes."[22] Other ancient sources share the importance of a cupbearer as well. "In Tobit, it is said that Esarhaddon's cupbearer [is] second only to him in his kingdom" (Tobit 1:22). The History of Herodotus (iii.34) states that "Cambyses [does] one of his friends a favor by appointing his son as cupbearer."[23] It is also worth noting that some scholars believe Nehemiah was a eunuch. Eunuchs commonly served as officials to the king because of the contact they would have with his harem.[24] It is clear Nehemiah has not received his position as cupbearer haphazardly but as a testament to his character and integrity. Though Nehemiah is in close proximity to the king, it is important to understand that Near Eastern monarchs are recognized as almost divine-like figures who would leave the people trembling in respect.[25] Nehemiah takes his service to God so seriously that he wants to be the best cupbearer he can be to honor the king as a part of his service to God. In Nehemiah 1:11b he records, "Now I was a cupbearer to the King." The Hebrew literally translates it as "now I [am] in charge of the wine."[26] When wine is placed in front of the king, it is the cupbearer's job to drink out of it first to make sure it is not poisoned.[27] Nehemiah would literally put his life on the line many occasions to serve the king. It is a common occurrence for the wealthy enemies

22. Ibid., 41.
23. Fensham, *Books of Ezra and Nehemiah*, 2117-18.
24. Ibid., 2119-23.
25. Brown, *Message of Nehemiah*, 41.
26. Fensham, *Books of Ezra and Nehemiah*, 2138-40.
27. Ibid.

of a king to try and poison him through bribery of a cupbearer. The cupbearer has to first sample the wine before the king by pouring it into his hands. Constant attempts to poison a king would leave the person suspicious and paranoid.[28]

Nehemiah's role as a cupbearer is stressed again in 2:1a: "In the month of Nisan, in the twentieth year of King Artaxerxes, when wine [is] before him, I [take] up the wine and [give] it to the king." Scholars speculate that Nehemiah waits for the ideal time to ask for his appeal during a festival when there is massive celebration throughout the land. One Greek historian explains that "no one who [asks] a boon that day at the king's board [shall be denied his request]."[29] Most likely, Nehemiah waits four months to make the big ask waiting for the ideal opportunity, which is why he looks miserable as everybody else is rejoicing for the new year:[30]

> And the king said to me, "Why is your face sad, seeing you are not sick? This is nothing but sadness of the heart." Then I was very much afraid. I said to the king, "Let the king live forever! Why should not my face be sad, when the city, the place of my fathers' graves, lies in ruins, and its gates have been destroyed by fire?" Then the king said to me, "What are you requesting?" So I prayed to the God of heaven. And I said to the king, "If it pleases the king, and if your servant has found favor in your sight, that you send me to Judah, to the city of my fathers' graves, that I may rebuild it." And the king said to me (the queen sitting beside him), "How long will you be gone, and when will you return?" So it pleased the king to send me when I had given him a time. And I said to the king, "If it pleases the king, let letters be given me to the governors of the province Beyond the River, that they may let me pass through until I come to Judah, and a letter to Asaph, the keeper of the king's forest, that he may give me timber to make beams for the gates of the fortress of the temple, and for the wall of the city, and for the house that I shall occupy."

---

28. Throntveit, *Ezra-Nehemiah*, 1451.
29. Brown, *Message of Nehemiah*, 45.
30. Ibid.

And the king granted me what I asked, for the good hand of my God was upon me.[31]

Based on dialogue between Nehemiah and King Artaxerxes, it is obvious that Nehemiah uses the four months of silence to methodically prepare and plan what he is going to ask for and say when it comes to rebuilding the gates, walls and other parts according to verses 7-8. Even though the king grants Nehemiah's request, Nehemiah takes time to thank God. Over the course of the book, the reader can see the ups and downs a cupbearer turned builder has in leading God's people to rebuilding Jerusalem.

Nehemiah and Amos are great examples of biblical leaders who have two totally different backgrounds and contexts but are still able to have dual vocations in their service to God. Nehemiah rubs shoulders with royalty and is in a palace in his service to God, and Amos is a herdsman and farmer of sycamore figs. Both carry out a service to God as a primary vocation while having a "day job" as well.

THE APOSTLE PAUL

The New Testament's most famous bi-vocational minister is the Apostle Paul. In fact, Paul's occupation as a "tentmaker" was the genesis for what has been commonly known as "tentmaking" in reference to those functioning as bi-vocational ministers. The biblical passage disclosing Paul's occupation is Acts 18:1-4, which states, "After this Paul left Athens and went to Corinth. And he found a Jew named Aquila, a native of Pontus, recently come from Italy with his wife Priscilla, because Claudius had commanded all the Jews to leave Rome. And he went to see them, and because he was of the same trade he stayed with them and worked, for they were tentmakers by trade. And he reasoned in the synagogue every Sabbath, and tried to persuade Jews and Greeks." Paul, as a tentmaker, would not have been too uncommon in the first-century religious context, for rabbis would often have to support them apart from

---

31. Neh 2:2-8.

the religious institution. Paul was falling in line with the rabbinical custom of combining one's study of the Torah with a marketable trade such as tentmaking.[32] Rabbi Judah says, "He that teaches not his son a trade is as if he taught him to be a thief." An unknown rabbi says, "He that has a trade in his hand is as a vineyard that is fenced."[33] This can easily explain Paul's affirming attitude of hard work when it comes to the study of Scripture, along with working his physical body in a trade.

Jewish rabbis were not the only ones who had dual roles, for outside of the Jewish religious context were Greco-Roman philosophers like Dio Chrysostom, who would charge fees and work in other occupations to make a living.[34] In fact, it was common for philosophers to use their workshops as environments for "intellectual activity." There, students would hear lectures, and people would engage in conversation. Such was the case with Simon the shoemaker, for the Cynic tradition suggests that Simon held philosophical conversations in his workshop with the likes of Pericles, Socrates and other intellectuals. The key virtue Cynics held was that of being self-sufficient, which is exactly what allowed Simon to have a trade that could support his philosophical, Socratic-Cynic teaching.[35]

The Apostle Paul was not merely functioning as a tentmaker prior to his conversion, but was even doing so during his ministry to the Gentiles. The actual translation of Paul's trade was "leather working," as indicated by the word when he is often referred to as "tentmaker," σκηνοποιός (skenopoios).[36] The New Testament scholar F. F. Bruce suggests: "This trade was closely connected with the principal product of Paul's native province, a cloth of goats' hair called cilicium, used for cloaks, curtains, and other fabrics designed to give protection against wet."[37] Bruce seems to get it

32. Ibid., 11.
33. Henry, *Commentary*, Acts 18:1–6.
34. Hock, *Social Context*, 67.
35. Ibid., 39.
36. Dorsett, *Developing Leadership Teams*, 306.
37. Bruce, *Book of Acts*, Acts 18, 346.

partially right, but does not give a full explanation of the Greek word *skenopoios*. *Skenopoios* in the most basic sense describes one who makes tents. But, the other nuances associated with *skenopoios* give the wider sense of one who works with leather, canvas, and linens. The word *skenopoios* is referred to as a *hapax legomenon*, because there are no other New Testament passages containing the same word.[38]

The early church fathers weighed in on the discussion of Paul's trade by offering different interpretations of *skenopoios*. Gregory of Nyssa translated this in his own way by giving the title "stitcher of tents" to Paul. Meanwhile Rufinus, Theodoret, and Chrysostom refer to Paul as a "shoemaker."[39] Origen translates *skenopoios* in what later became the accepted sense of tentmaker. Also, Origen classically gives an allegorical image that compares how Peter, Andrew, and the sons of Zebedee where transformed from being fishermen to "fishers of people," and it is in this same way that Paul's occupation was transformed to tentmaker. Prior to Paul's conversion, Origen believed he was building merely physical tents. However, post-conversion, Paul was building tents much like the ones Israel would use in the desert to contain Yahweh's presence. This was synonymous with Paul's passion for planting congregations.[40]

Regardless, the point is made that the Apostle Paul worked with his hands, and most tents in Paul's setting were made of leather. Although a tentmaker, Paul would not have been limited to that professional specialty alone; he would have made other products from his overall training with leather working. If so, Paul would have gone through in-depth training as a young boy, starting as an apprentice around the age of thirteen under his father. The training would have been for an intense time period of two or three years, with the hope he would become impeccable at his trade by the age of fifteen or sixteen.[41] There is the likelihood that the tents

38. Keller, "Luke's Narration," 441.
39. Hock, *Social Context*, 20-21.
40. Martin and Oden, *Acts*, 224-25.
41. Hock, *Social Context*, 24.

and leather items that he made would have been of such great importance to the Roman army that it would have afforded Paul and his family dual citizenship.[42] The art of tentmaking would have afforded Paul the opportunity to perform his trade as a missionary, giving him the opportunity to be able to carry his own portable tools with him on his travels. His tools would have included a variety of knives and awls that could be used to cut and sew leather. His essential toolkit allowed him to travel freely on his missionary journeys. It is this that would have expanded Paul's social life, allowing him to have interactions with many different people who were both Jewish and Gentile as he labored in his workshop.[43]

It is not a coincidence that Paul met his two key ministry partners in Corinth, where they too were practicing the trade of tentmaking. Paul's connections with Priscilla and Aquila were pivotal in their business together, and it also provided Paul with a hospitable home in which to stay. Acts 18:1-4 suggests that during the week Paul was working as a tentmaking laborer, and on the weekends he was preaching in the synagogues.[44] What he was doing as a first-century Christian was no different than some of the Jews of influence in his social context. Take Paul's rabbinic teacher, Hillel, for instance. His occupation was woodcutting, and even Shammai, who was Hillel's rival, worked as a carpenter.[45]

One may wonder why and how this is pertinent to Paul's tentmaking. There is a strong likelihood that Paul used his workshop in much the same way, that is to say, for entering into conversations with his coworkers and customers about the gospel, in order to win people for Christ.[46] When Chrysostom reflects on Paul's tentmaking, he says, "For being raised as an unceasing worker is the nature of philosophy."[47] Chrysostom has possibly offered some corrective here, in that he points out that those who are wise and

---

42. Witherington, *1 and 2 Thessalonians*, 1 Thess 2:9, 38.
43. Hock, *Social Context*, 25.
44. Dorsett, *Developing Leadership Teams*, 320.
45. Vincent, *Word Studies*, Acts 18:3.
46. Ibid., 41.
47. Martin and Oden, *Acts*, 223.

Biblical Precedents for Bi-vocational Ministry

intellectual were not necessarily the ones born in privileged families, but those that could toil with sweat beading down their brows.

A. Deissman, a late eighteenth-century German theologian, held a unique view within New Testament scholarship regarding Paul and his occupation as a tentmaker. Deissman was so intrigued with Paul's tentmaking occupation that he believed that even some of Paul's letters were probably written from his workshop. Like the prophet Amos, Deissman believed that Paul easily identified himself with those who were of lower class and in poverty.[48] Paul's long hours on the job probably did not equate to a large salary. If we imagined Paul as living in today's North American context, we might say that his money went to pay for rent, food, and clothing, and there still may have been times in his life in which he could not make ends meet.[49]

Other noted scriptural evidence of Paul's bi-vocational status is found in his First and Second Letters to the Thessalonians. First Thessalonians 2:9 states, "For you remember, brothers, our labor and toil: we worked night and day, that we might not be a burden to any of you, while we proclaimed to you the gospel of God." Paul's work came to be known for the Thessalonians as a model for them to imitate, which fueled his working "night and day." Paul indicates the reason for this work by saying that he does not want to be a "burden" to them.[50]

Another passage that highlights Paul's bi-vocational ministry elucidates a few different reasons why he worked as a tentmaker. Paul states in 2 Thessalonians 3:7-10, "For you yourselves know how you ought to imitate us, because we were not idle when we were with you, nor did we eat anyone's bread without paying for it, but with toil and labor we worked night and day, that we might not be a burden to any of you. It was not because we do not have that right, but to give you in ourselves an example to imitate. For even when we were with you, this we commanded you, 'If any will not work, neither let him eat.'" Perhaps, another reason was to have

---

48. Hock, *Social Context*, 14.
49. Ibid., 31.
50. Fee, "First Word for the Disruptive-Idle," 5949.

a teaching moment with his Gentile converts, who may not have had a strong work ethic or could have even looked down on people who had to support themselves through manual labor. This is further evidenced in 2 Thessalonians 4:11, where Paul says, "Work with your hands, as we instructed you." A common theme for these converts appears to be idleness.[51] Paul's occupation allowed him to be viewed as a diligent worker in his social context, which his converts could emulate. Richard Hocks states it well when he says, "By placing Paul in the workshop—that is, by taking seriously the fact that Paul was a tentmaker—we have located him more precisely in the social and intellectual milieu of the urban center of the Greek East of the early empire."[52] To view Paul as a theologian who only spent his time in synagogues is to get a blurred look, because it does not take seriously who he was within his social context.

PAUL'S ROMAN CITIZENSHIP COMBINED WITH HIS TENTMAKING

It is hard to deny the Apostle Paul's contribution to early Christianity as the first Christian missionary. The fruits of Paul's labor are remarkable because of the power of the Holy Spirit in his life and the boldness that he possessed. However, one of the dimensions of Paul that is often neglected or debated is his Roman citizenship. Paul's Roman citizenship aided him in preaching the gospel because of the rights that came with it. Paul's rights helped him travel, saved him from death, and protected his converts, which are seen in three separate passages in the book of Acts. Though some may not believe in Paul's Roman citizenship, it is clear that this denial ultimately disrupts the later part of the book of Acts.

Paul's Roman citizenship is referred to three separate times in Acts 16:35-39, 22:22-29, and 25:6-12. These passages for the most part remain undisputed. However, some scholars due to historical evidence doubt Paul's Roman citizenship. On the opposite end of

---

51. Hock, *Social Context*, 45.
52. Ibid., 68.

the spectrum, there are some scholars who say that for the purpose of the narrative the issue of citizenship was conjured by the author. This extreme view suggests that around the end of the first century the aim of the author was to exhibit the gospel's international claims. A rabbinic Jew would no better fit this claim than Paul who is Roman. The early church and the interpretation of Acts come under unique complications due to the sentiments of scholars regarding the Roman citizenship of Paul.[53]

One of the main issues that comes out of dealing with the subject of Paul's Roman citizenship has to do with either the likelihood or the credibleness that during the midpoint of the first century Paul was a Roman citizen despite his social and cultural position as a Jew. Many scholars have voiced before this argument. Regardless of how many occasions this argument has been mentioned there are those who hold an extreme view that still remains unchanged. The cruciality of Paul's Roman citizenship and its historicity remain untouched, no matter the numerous arguments for the likelihood or the credibleness that Paul was a Roman citizen despite his social and cultural position as a Jew.[54]

The structure to the final part of Acts is affected overall due to the passages regarding Paul's Roman citizenship. In discussing this topic, there must be attention given to the passages in Acts, especially Acts 16:35-39, where Paul's Roman citizenship creates a shift in the narrative regarding Silas's and Paul's own fate:[55]

> But when it was day, the magistrates sent the police, saying, "Let those men go." And the jailer reported these words to Paul, saying, "The magistrates have sent to let you go. Therefore come out now and go in peace." But Paul said to them, "They have beaten us publicly, uncondemned, men who are Roman citizens, and have thrown us into prison; and do they now throw us out secretly? No! Let them come themselves and take us out." The police reported these words to the magistrates, and

---

53. Witherington, *New Testament History*, 5027.
54. Witherington, *Paul Quest*, 846.
55. Witherington, *New Testament History*, 5878.

they were afraid when they heard that they were Roman citizens. So they came and apologized to them. And they took them out and asked them to leave the city.

As citizens of Rome, Paul and Silas were both free from any type of Jewish form of punishment according to both Porcian and Valerian Laws, which would include crucifixion, beatings with rods, scourging, and other forms of punishment that would have been considered humiliating.[56] Under the Valerian and Porcian laws, a Roman citizen had the right to a fair hearing in the presence of a Roman magistrate but must also be formally charged, penalized, and accused. The question arises in this situation as to why Paul did not communicate that he was a Roman citizen before he and Silas were beaten? It may be the case that the magistrates were in such an irate state that Paul had no chance to do so.[57] In verse 39, something interesting occurs where an official apology is demanded by Paul, possibly asked for in hopes of discouraging any persecution that would occur to his new converts. A role reversal of power occurred when Paul accepted the apology after he had been beaten, and this happened to be following the salvation of the households in Philippi. However, this apology may be out of fear as well because those that were in office would have received stiff penalties for directly disregarding the protection given by citizenship.[58] The magistrates tried to right the wrong that they committed because they knew that they would be held directly accountable for their actions, if what they did came to the attention of certain persons in positions of authority. "Under the *Lex Julia* on public violence anyone who, while holding *imperium* or office, puts to death or flogs a Roman citizen contrary to his [right of] appeal or orders any of the aforementioned things to be done, or puts [a yoke] on his neck so that he may be captured."[59]

---

56. Rapske, *Book of Acts*, 299.
57. Ibid.
58. Ibid., 429.
59. Ibid., 52.

Biblical Precedents for Bi-vocational Ministry

PAUL AND THE ROMAN TRIBUNE

The next passage is from Acts 22:22-29. In this passage, a Roman tribune is going to flog Paul:

> Up to this word they listened to him. Then they raised their voices and said, "Away with such a fellow from the earth! For he should not be allowed to live." And as they were shouting and throwing off their cloaks and flinging dust into the air, the tribune ordered him to be brought into the barracks, saying that he should be examined by flogging, to find out why they were shouting against him like this. But when they had stretched him out for the whips, Paul said to the centurion who was standing by, "Is it lawful for you to flog a man who is a Roman citizen and uncondemned?" When the centurion heard this, he went to the tribune and said to him, "What are you about to do? For this man is a Roman citizen." So the tribune came and said to him, "Tell me, are you a Roman citizen?" And he said, "Yes." The tribune answered, "I bought this citizenship for a large sum." Paul said, "But I am a citizen by birth." So those who were about to examine him withdrew from him immediately, and the tribune also was afraid, for he realized that Paul was a Roman citizen and that he had bound him.

According to verse 28, the tribune, Claudius Lysias, for his own Roman citizenship, paid a large sum of money. Due to Paul's response of being a Roman citizen, Claudius Lysias was stricken with fear and had a change of heart toward Paul. Claudius Lysias acted upon Paul's behalf as reported in Acts 23:26-30 because of Paul's claim of Roman citizenship. Immediately following Claudius Lysias's statement of paying for Roman citizenship, Paul speaks of how through his parents he has rights to citizenship. Any false claims of citizenship would result in death, so a person claiming such status was usually believed. Perhaps, Paul is most likely believed because such a serious claim if false would result in his death. The first century BC would have to be the time that dates back to when the Roman citizenship is granted to this specific

Jewish family.[60] Dating back to 171 BC it was according to Ramsay that Pompey allowed some Jews who had become citizens of Tarsus to also receive Roman citizenship. There is also a later tradition recorded by Jerome that Mark Antony rewarded the parents of Paul with Roman citizenship (who arrived to Tarsus from Gischala) because of a service that was performed for Mark Antony.[61] By some, Paul is viewed as a part of an upper class because of his citizenship and the education that he would have received. Because of this citizenship, scholar William Ramsay said that he would have taken Paul's Roman citizenship as "proof that his family was one of distinction and at best moderate wealth."[62]

Paul was accustomed to persecutions under Roman magistrates where he had been beaten with rods three times and under Jewish authority was lashed thirty-nine times on five occasions (2 Cor 9:30; 11:24-25; 16:22-24). Through these situations Paul experienced great physical pain, but Paul could have been able to get out of these punishments as well with his rights as a Roman citizen. In these other situations, Paul welcomed the persecution; however, in the particular punishment of flogging Paul claims his Roman citizen rights.[63] Perhaps the lashing and beatings with rods could not be compared to the punishment of flogging. Being killed or usually crippled would be the result of such a punishment. Therefore, Paul was facing a possible death that was unjust.

PAUL APPEALS TO THE EMPEROR

Acts 25:6-12 is the third passage concerning the subject of Paul's Roman citizenship:

> After he stayed among them not more than eight or ten days, he went down to Caesarea. And the next day he took his seat on the tribunal and ordered Paul to be

---

60. Ibid., 144.
61. Ibid., 80.
62. Hock, "Paul's Tentmaking," 557.
63. Rapske, *Book of Acts*, 56.

brought. When he had arrived, the Jews who had come down from Jerusalem stood around him, bringing many and serious charges against him that they could not prove. Paul argued in his defense, "Neither against the law of the Jews, nor against the temple, nor against Caesar have I committed any offense." But Festus, wishing to do the Jews a favor, said to Paul, "Do you wish to go up to Jerusalem and there be tried on these charges before me?" But Paul said, "I am standing before Caesar's tribunal, where I ought to be tried. To the Jews I have done no wrong, as you yourself know very well. If then I am a wrongdoer and have committed anything for which I deserve to die, I do not seek to escape death. But if there is nothing to their charges against me, no one can give me up to them. I appeal to Caesar." Then Festus, when he had conferred with his council, answered, "To Caesar you have appealed; to Caesar you shall go."

Paul is requesting to be turned over to the hands of the emperor in Rome instead of being punished in Jerusalem by his Jewish accusers. The only people who were believed to opt for such a decision as Paul had made were Roman citizens. Paul's appeal is allowed because the governor had no choice. There was no verdict announced of Paul being guilty. Paul's motivation seemed to be that he would rather take his risk with being under the judgment of the Roman law, instead of risking it with the Jewish authorities where he would not get fair treatment.[64] In the latter portions of Acts (26:32; 28:19) there is reference made to the appeal requested by Paul to the emperor. An appeal to the emperor for a Roman citizen facing a severe penalty was of great consideration because it could place the citizen with a tribunal that was more gracious, unbiased, and could ultimately rescue them from punishment that they would likely receive elsewhere.[65]

There is much consideration to be taken that Paul indeed was a Roman citizen. For instance his Greco-Roman rhetoric and display of well-known philosophy such as Stoicism give credence

64. Ibid., 183.
65. Ibid., 55.

that this was an intelligent person that was familiar with matters outside of the Jewish realm. There are in fact many references to Jews who were Roman citizens prior to the midpoint of the first century AD. As a citizen of Tarsus, it was likely for Paul to also be a citizen of Rome, giving citizenship to him in a couple of cities. A possible means of execution for a Roman citizen was beheading, and church tradition records this was the means by which Paul was executed by the Roman authorities, validating that Paul indeed was a Roman citizen. Ramsay wrote about how a Roman name was given to every Roman citizen and to adhere to one's legal rights the citizen would have to use their full and proper Roman names that were designated to them. A personal name, a surname, and a family name were the three names that citizens were given. There were only fifteen possible names that would be given for a personal name (*praenomen*), the name of the most relatives was the surname (*nomen* or *gentilicium*) that associated the citizen to them, and the individual's name was the family name (*cogenomen*). If the three parts of Paul's Roman name were recorded, it would limit the skeptics of his citizenship. However, it must be considered that all three names of any Roman citizen are not recorded in the New Testament anywhere.[66]

ROMAN CITIZENSHIP FOR THE GOSPEL'S SAKE

Throughout Paul's writings, he nowhere specifically gives mention to his Roman citizenship, which seems pointless to some scholars to discuss. However, the accounts in Acts regarding this topic of citizenship should not be neglected. It seems that Paul is hesitant to speak about this citizenship, except for when it is able to save his life for the sake of spreading the gospel or to reach a certain destination. Paul had many opportunities to go before the emperor and witness because of the rights of appeal process that he acted upon. Paul tried not to jeopardize his witness among the Jews, and that perhaps motivated him to keep his Roman citizenship quiet.

---

66. Ibid., 84.

Roman citizenship to Paul was not the most important thing to him, which would give reason for his leaving this detail out of his writings. Paul wrote as an apostle of Christ, not as a Roman citizen. He kept the spotlight on Christ, which was exactly the message his converts needed to hear. It seems that Paul did not want his title to get in the way of advancing the gospel. Rather, he wanted the gospel itself to be the driving force in reaching Jews and Gentiles. Paul used his Roman citizenship not for bragging rights, but as a well-crafted tool that would allow him freedom to travel and preach. As an evangelist, Paul would have been able to enter cities in the Roman colony because of the rights he would be able to claim as a Roman. As a Roman citizen, there would be honor paid to him as seen in the passages of Acts. With this honor was also an allowance to travel with other citizens on Roman routes. One of such places was Spain, where Paul wanted to travel, and the only possibility for such a voyage was due to his citizenship. Paul claimed to be all things to all people—to the Jews he was a Jew and to the Gentiles he was a Gentile. Roman citizenship would have been his common thread in relating to the Gentiles.[67]

Amos, Nehemiah, and Paul are very similar in their hard work as bi-vocational ministers for the Lord. They are humble in their vocations as laborers, but glorified in their work for God. They are examples of how the people of God can be used in everyday work to accomplish extraordinary measures for God.

---

67. Witherington, *New Testament History*, 5987.

5

Lessons from Early Revivalists

FOR THE UNITED METHODIST Church to experience revival it must develop and recontextualize the order of elder, by revisiting its early history with lay preachers and bi-vocational ministers such as John Nelson, Jacob Albright, Martin Boehm and Richard Allen. These men of God worked with their hands as tile-makers, farmers, and stonemasons but were used by God to help lead a movement. The key for the future of the United Methodist Church is not to develop a new model for doing ministry in the twenty-first century, but to once again discover who Methodists were from their genesis.

In the early years of Methodism, John Wesley was not a strong advocate for lay preachers because he wanted his preachers to have proper training and to be ordained by the Church of England. Wesley's staunch view of lay preachers came to a culmination after the conversion of Thomas Maxfield. Maxfield, was converted under Wesley's preaching in 1739 in Bristol. Wesley reports that Maxfield had a religious experience that was characterized as "violent," which in context could be understood as radical. It was so transformative that a year later in 1740, Maxfield took the initiative to preach in Wesley's absence to the Foundery Society, which he had been left to shepherd. Upon Wesley's arrival back to the Foundery, he was quite shocked to find out that Maxfield had been preaching and complained to his mother Susanna who had been living in the Foundery. Wesley said, "'Thomas Maxfield has turned

Preacher, I find.' Susanna's response was, 'Take care what you do with respect to that young man, for he is as surely called of God to preach, as you are. Examine what have been the fruits of his preaching, and hear him also yourself.' Wesley bowed before the force of truth, and could only say, 'It is the Lord: let him do what seemeth him good.'"[1] This shows even Wesley acknowledged that God is the ultimate authority in a believer's life.

JOHN NELSON (1707-1770)

It was precisely this interaction that changed Wesley's mind about lay preachers, and while things did not exactly work out with Maxfield in the long run, due to theological conflicts between the two, it did pave the way for a bi-vocational preacher by the name of John Nelson (1707-1770). Like Maxfield, Nelson was converted under the preaching of John Wesley, but he was converted in Moorfields. Nelson described his conversion experience in his journal:

> His countenance struck such an awful dread upon me, before I heard him speak, that it made my heart beat like the pendulum of a clock; and when he did speak, I thought his whole discourse was aimed at me. When he had done, I said, "This man can tell the secrets of my heart; he hath fully described the disease of my heart, but he hath not left me there, for he hath shown the remedy, even the blood of Jesus." Then was my soul filled with consolation through hope.[2]

Nelson's salvation experience made him question his life's call and the direction that he felt God was taking him. Immediately, the people who were living with him in London did not want him around because of his enthusiasm about his conversion, so they kicked him out. Also, his foreman wanted him to work on the first Saturday after his conversion, but Nelson did not respond well to this. He wanted to honor God with the Sabbath and not work.

---

1. Heitzenrater, *Wesley and the People*, 115.
2. Nelson, *Extract of John Nelson's Journal*, 14.

Ministry Makeover

Although Nelson was not fired, he decided to leave his job as well as London to make his trek back to Yorkshire. His heart could not bear the thought of his friends, family and loved ones not hearing the gospel. Nelson dismissed the thought of how he turned his back on guaranteed income in London.[3] When he returned to Yorkshire, he entered bi-vocational ministry. During the day, he worked as a stonemason, while in the evenings he saw many people come to faith through his preaching.[4]

As John Nelson engaged in his bi-vocational ministry and saw the fruit of his labor for the Lord, he became eager to meet up with Wesley during Wesley's next pass through Bristol. Nelson repeatedly invited Wesley to come and witness what the Lord was doing. Wesley was shocked when he arrived in Bristol. He recorded:

> In May, on the repeated invitation of John Nelson, who had been for some time calling sinners to repentance at Bristol, and the adjoining town in the West Riding of Yorkshire, I went to Bristol, and found his labor had not been in vain. Many of the greatest profligates in all the country were now changed. Their blasphemies were turned to praise. Many of the most abandoned drunkards were now sober: many Sabbath-breakers remembered the Sabbath to keep it holy. The whole town wore a new face. Such a change did God work by the artless testimony of one plain man! . . . Perhaps in no part of England has Methodism flourished more than in that region where Nelson first cast the prolific seed.[5]

The harvest that John Nelson's bi-vocational ministry was reaping was an unprecedented revival reminiscent of the early church. Unfortunately for Nelson, and like it had been for the apostles of the early church, Nelson experienced intense persecution as he travelled through areas like Leeds, Lancashire, Chesire, and other territories. Along with the exhausting journeys themselves, it was not uncommon for him to encounter hostile mobs

---

3. Ibid., 37.
4. Nelson, *Lives of Early Methodist Preachers*, 92.
5. Nelson, *Extract of John Nelson's Journal*, vi.

that thought his Methodist message was a threat to the statuesque religious communities. They were also not accustomed to a bi-vocational minister.

Such was the case when Nelson arrived to preach at Ackham, where two men approached him who had been contracted to kill him. They severely beat him to the point that the two men claimed they killed him in order to collect their reward.[6] It did not stop there, because other antagonists physically assaulted Nelson and hurled verbal insults at him about his doctrine, on Easter Sunday![7] Nelson recalled hearing this as his aggressors were leaving the scene: "It is impossible for him to live; and if John Wesley comes on Tuesday, we will kill him: then we should be quite rid of the Methodists forever; for no one will dare to come if they two be killed."[8] Wesley shared the courage displayed by Nelson, who after getting the proper attention from a surgeon for the wound on his head went back out preaching right away.[9]

If Nelson's oppressors could not kill him, they would cleverly plot against him by strong-arming him to become a soldier. They captured him one day after he had preached to a congregation in Adwalton.[10] Nelson refused to wear the uniform of a soldier, so his captors took him to Bradford, and threw him into a dark dungeon. This only propelled Nelson's fame even more throughout England. Nelson stood his ground and said, "I shall not fight; for I cannot bow my knee before the Lord, to pray for a man, and get up and kill him when I have done; for I know God both hears me speak and sees me act; and I should expect the lot of the hypocrite, if my actions contradict my prayers."[11] In addition to the physical abuse and isolation, one sergeant even resorted to bribery to no avail in trying to get Nelson to put on the uniform. On July 28, 1744,

---

6. Ibid., 197.
7. Ibid., 199.
8. Ibid.
9. Wesley, *Works of John Wesley*, 3:11282.
10. Nelson, *Extract of John Nelson's Journal*, 124.
11. Ibid., 138.

Nelson finally received his discharge. He travelled to Newcastle, and returned to preaching God's Word.[12]

Nelson was not the only one who suffered persecution; his wife did as well. While in Leeds she was heinously victimized by an angry mob of women simply because of her husband's preaching. The worst part about the whole encounter was that she was visibly pregnant. Shockingly, the mob of women did not care and beat her so badly that it resulted in a miscarriage. The Nelsons persevered, and John Nelson said about his wife, "This treatment she has reason to remember to her life's end; but God more than made it up to her by filling her heart with peace and love."[13]

JACOB ALBRIGHT (1759–1808)

Another bi-vocational minister who was pivotal to Methodism was Jacob Albright (1759–1808) who was born into Lutheranism in Douglass Township, Pennsylvania. Albright's faith became refined with fire through tragedy, as several of his children died of dysentery in 1790. This left him broken, but open to the power of the Holy Spirit.[14] Albright sought worship opportunities in the Lutheran and Reformed churches. Unfortunately, it only left him in a constant state of depression without any assurance of salvation.[15] Albright gave a description of his prior faith journey by saying, "We knew nothing of conversation; there no trace of prayer-meetings, Bible study, family prayers, Sunday-schools or revivals. Hardly a show of godliness remained. The power thereof was outlawed as fanaticism. The salt had lost its savor."[16] This was the case in Albright's Christian experience until he interacted with a few evangelistic groups, one of which was the Methodists, who were already significantly impacting the Pennsylvania-German

---

12. Ibid., 171.
13. Ibid., 105.
14. Joyner, *Unofficial United Methodist Handbook*, 671.
15. Yrigoyen and Warrick, *Historical Dictionary of Methodism*, 87.
16. Kinghorn, *Heritage of American Methodism*, 87.

territory. Prior to his "genuine conversion" experience in 1791 at the age of thirty-three, he described his prior spiritual state as "a walk frivolously in the path of a carnal life with little thought about the object of human life."[17] Albright's visit with Adam Riegel, a United Brethren in Christ lay preacher, was instrumental for his conversion. Albright stated as he articulated his own conversion experience:

> In a place of a worldly-minded spirit I was filled with a holy love for God and for his true children. All depression of spirit was removed; sweet comfort and deep peace permeated my being; the Spirit of God witnessed that I was a child of God; one wave of joy after another swept over my soul and such ecstasy thrilled me as cannot be described. In comparison with this all sinful pleasures and enjoyments were emptiness and vanity. My prayer was answered. My world was filled with gratitude and praise to God, the Giver of every good and perfect gift.[18]

After his conversion, Albright's quest for deeper spiritual discipline and learning led him to a class meeting led by a Methodist named Isaac Davis. Albright's newfound faith and his connection with the Methodists helped him grow. He practiced the Christian disciplines, participated in the means of grace, and learned foundational Christian truths. Also, on a practical note, Albright, who was primarily a German speaker, started to learn English. He became so confident that he began to preach and teach in the Methodist class meeting as a licensed exhorter. This only led Albright to desire to share the gospel with the German people. In Albright's opinion, the more established Christian churches, like those in the Lutheran, Reformed, and Mennonite traditions, were the "great decline of religion."[19]

In order to carry out Albright's call to reach his German neighbors, he connected with like-minded people, including Martin Boehm and Wilhelm Otterbein, who sought to connect with the

---

17. Good, "Albright College Sesquicentennial."
18. Kinghorn, *Heritage of American Methodism*, 88.
19. Ibid.

widespread revival of which the Methodists were a part. Naturally, they tried to express their desire to reach the German-speakers in their region to Bishop Francis Asbury, the predominant ecclesiastical leader of the movement. Asbury did not share the same vision for communicating the gospel in the German people's vernacular. As a result, Albright went on a solo journey to bring the gospel to his native people, while Boehm and Otterbein started their own work, which would later become the United Brethren in Christ Church.[20] Albright described the call he felt to reach his German-speaking brethren. "I frequently cast myself upon my knees and pleaded with hot tears that God might lead my German brethren to a knowledge of the truth as it is in Jesus, and might send them faithful leaders, who should preach to them the gospel in power, awaken lifeless professors of religion, and lead them to a life of true godliness, so that they might be made partakers of the peace of God and of the inheritance of the saints in light. Thus I prayed daily."[21] Albright still felt a strong affinity for Methodism despite not having a formal connection with its widespread membership. He practiced the Discipline and Articles of Faith as his religious polity.[22] Albright started to educate himself when it came to ministry and his new task as an itinerant preacher. Many noted the success of his ministry, but like John Nelson, he underwent persecutions. He was physically threatened, attacked by mobs, and had stones thrown at him while riding on horseback. All of this was coupled with the fact he was bi-vocational.[23] Albright was referred to as "an honest tile maker" and farmer.[24] He took his personal faith so seriously that he wanted his vocation as a tile maker to honor God to the best of his ability, which is why he tried to perfect the art of tile-making in order to make the best possible product.[25]

---

20. Ibid.
21. Ibid., 88.
22. Miller, *Short Description*, 4.
23. Ibid.
24. Joyner, *United Methodist Questions*, 319.
25. Ibid.

Lessons from Early Revivalists

Despite his juggling act, Albright had great success at maintaining his tile business, farming, and providing for his family while carrying out his calling to share the gospel. He loved his family and valued his strong sense of familial duties, while carrying out his duties as an itinerant preacher. Albright was a great leader, not only to his converts, but also to his family, to the point that the farm and tile business were run primarily by his wife and children.[26]

Albright's success can be attributed to his faithfulness in small beginnings. He was not concerned about the size of his congregation. Whether it was in an open field or a house, he would preach to the best of his ability, empowered by the work of the Holy Spirit. Since he had a willingness to preach whenever and wherever, without a systematic approach, his converts were scattered in many geographical locations. It is quite miraculous that his converts joined together to form anything resembling a denomination. In fact, in the 1790s Albright tried to gather some representatives from his movement for a meeting, and only five people attended. Much like Wesley, Albright never had the intent to start his own denomination, but he knew there needed to be a structure to govern the movement.

Albright's followers conducted their first General Conference in 1803, where they ordained Albright as their leader or bishop. However, he did not refer to himself as bishop but primarily as a pastor. After this organization, Albright continued his high impact pace of itinerancy, leading a growing movement, working as a tile-maker/farmer, and being a family man, which ultimately led to burnout.[27]

This high level of activity led to his death from tuberculosis at the young age of forty-nine. Though his ministry was short-lived, his impact has lasted well over two centuries.[28] Actually, the total time Albright spent in ministry was only an astounding twelve years.[29] The ironic part of his story is that his followers, who formed the Evangelical Association, were grafted into the

---

26. Good, "Albright College Sesquicentennial."
27. Ibid.
28. Joyner, *United Methodist Questions*, 319.
29. Yrigoyen and Warrick, *Historical Dictionary of Methodism*, 12.

United Methodist Church's merger in 1968. In a sense, Albright did join Asbury, not in the eighteenth century, but later in the twentieth century with this new union.[30] The remarkable thing about Albright's leadership, unlike Wesley with the Methodists, or Otterbein and Boehm with the United Brethren Church, was that Albright carried the load for the Evangelicals as their sole leader.[31]

MARTIN BOEHM (1725-1812)

Another leader who emerged from humble beginnings and worked as a bi-vocational minister in the Methodist movement was Martin Boehm (1725–1812). Like Albright, Boehm was born in Pennsylvania and raised as a German-speaking Mennonite. Growing up in a strict Mennonite home, Boehm was baptized, learned doctrine, and joined the church. However, Boehm felt like he simply had a religious upbringing and not a vital and personal relationship with Christ. The self-realization of Boehm's lack of spirituality was emphasized on the fateful day when his Mennonite congregation needed a pastor. They decided to cast lots, which was a Mennonite custom, and Boehm was selected to be the pastor.

Boehm was scared to death, because up to this point he was content managing his four-hundred–acre farm.[32] As a quiet farmer, Boehm was not used to public speaking, especially preaching. It is recorded that he would "stammer out a few words and then be obligated to sit down in shame and remorse."[33] This disappointment led him to desperation, which spurred him to cry out to God during the early months after he became a pastor because he knew deep down he was not a true believer. One day, as Boehm was working his fields, he sought the Lord in prayer. While praying, something dramatic happened that changed his life forever. Boehm knelt down while plowing the fields at the end of each row and prayed.

---

30. Good, "Albright College Sesquicentennial."
31. Kinghorn, *Heritage of American Methodism*, 87.
32. Joyner, *United Methodist Questions*, 673.
33. "Story of Boehm and Otterbein."

As Boehm prayed, the word "Lost" was repeated in his mind. Then, he fell on his knees in the middle of the fields and praised the Lord as Luke 19:10 came to his memory, "I have come to seek and save that which is lost." Boehm's life was forever changed.[34]

Boehm's conversion experience ignited his preaching for the rest of his ministry as he preached on repentance and faith. On the following Sunday, many in his congregation were converted by his preaching. Soon word spread to the other Mennonite congregations of Boehm's revivalist preaching. He began to preach wherever the Holy Spirit led him, whether it was in a church, someone's home, or even a barn. Boehm would hold revival services that were attended by a variety of people. These revivals were called "Great Meetings," and sometimes they lasted for a few days. Despite these meetings being conducted in Boehm's native language of German, it did not stop the English-speaking Methodists from attending and joining what God was doing in their midst.[35]

One of the most famous of these Great Meetings took place in 1767 in a barn in Lancaster, Pennsylvania, known as Isaac's Long Barn. It is a landmark in the history of United Methodism, because of an encounter that birthed a denomination. One thousand people were gathered in the barn on that fateful day as Boehm was preaching. However, there was one particular man, a Dutch Reformed pastor, who was deeply moved, Philipp William Otterbein. Immediately after Boehm concluded his sermon, Otterbein eagerly introduced himself by giving Boehm a huge hug and declaring "*Wir sind Brüder*" ("We are Brethren").[36] Many were touched by this scene of brotherhood and did not know at the time they were witnessing not only the beginning of a close friendship, but also the beginning of the Church of the United Brethren in Christ, co-founded by Boehm and Otterbein. In 1800, a General Conference was held to make the denomination official, and both Boehm and Otterbein were elected as the first bishops. Even from the beginning of this newly formed denomination, the United Brethren in

---

34. Ibid.
35. Kinghorn, *Heritage of American Methodism*, 81.
36. Ibid.

Christ felt themselves kin to Methodists, especially regarding the doctrine and discipline. In fact, it was a Methodist, Bishop Francis Asbury, who shared words at both Boehm and Otterbein's funerals when they died only one year apart in 1812 and 1813, both at the age of eighty-seven.[37]

Speaking about Boehm, Francis Asbury once said, "As the head of a family, a father, a neighbor, a friend, a companion, the prominent feature of his character was goodness; you felt that he was good. His mind was strong, and well stored with the learning necessary for one whose aim is to preach Christ with apostolic zeal and simplicity."[38] Boehm's hard work ethic as a farmer allowed him to be acclimated to the preaching settings of local barns. His humbleness of spirit and desire to see people won to Christ allowed God to use him in a powerful way. Though he was a layman, a farmer, and was uneducated, these things did not deter his ministry. His desire for a spirit of unity made up for any deficiencies he had as he worked within the body of Christ.

In looking back at the early Methodist history, one can see how it produced capable laity who were called by God and were empowered to do significant work for the kingdom of God. For the United Methodist Church to return to a movement, it will take giving the church back to the laity and bi-vocational pastors. People who are willing to work hard for the Lord and who provide for their loved ones. Their entire families and not just the individual leaders make sacrifices. God desires to return to using the tile-makers, farmers, and stonemasons of today.

RICHARD ALLEN (1760-1831)

Richard Allen (1760–1831) was his generation's Martin Luther King Jr. with a prophetic voice. Allen was a bi-vocational Methodist minister and circuit rider who also founded the first independent African Methodist Church, Bethel, that later led to the

---

37. "Story of Boehm and Otterbein."
38. Ibid.

birthing of the African Methodist Episcopal (AME) Church.[39] Allen was born to enslaved parents in 1760 in Philadelphia. In 1777, at the age of seventeen, he was converted to Christianity by the preaching of a Methodist minister. Soon after his conversion, Allen accepted his call to ministry. Allen's first sermon was to his slave master who was converted after Allen bought his freedom back. Immediately, Allen began his Methodist circuit rider career in humble beginnings without any money and not even having a formal education that allowed him to read. In fact, some believed that Allen was illiterate his entire life. Later in his life, at the time the AME Church elected Allen as its first bishop, it was Allen's literate grandson who would take notes for him and accompany Allen to all his meetings.[40]

Allen was known for being a reformer and entrepreneur. Allen's unique experiences allowed him to accompany General Washington's army where he hauled supplies for them while preaching the entire travels. Allen's bi-vocational ministry was in starting a boot and shoe business along with being a wagoner, a chimney sweep and a whole host of enterprises.[41]

Despite facing and fighting racism his entire life, Allen started a movement whether he realized it or not. Allen's reputation started to grow among Methodists as he was preaching in territories like New Jersey, Delaware, and Pennsylvania. The ironic part of his circuit was the white folks who would gather to hear his preaching and were in awe of the man of God. Francis Asbury, one of the first bishops of the newly formed Methodist Episcopal Church, learned about Richard Allen and desired to meet him. Asbury invited Allen to do a circuit with him into the southern parts of the country. Unfortunately, while in the throws of ministry Asbury cautioned "that Allen not intermix with slaves, and due to Allen's color, Allen would spend most nights in Asbury's carriage. Though the two parted as friends, Allen refused Asbury's offer, and in February of

---

39. PBS, "Richard Allen."
40. Simmons and Thomas, *Preaching with Sacred Fire*, 105.
41. Ibid.

1786 went to Philadelphia and St. George's."[42] St. George's received Allen to preach on one stipulation, which was only if he agreed to preach at the 5:00 a.m. service, the only time African Americans were allowed to have their own service and preacher. In Allen's mind, he thought the arrangement would only last a few weeks, but before he realized what was happening, the congregation started to grow, and what was meant to only last a few weeks, spanned for years. In one of his memoirs, as he reflected on his early days at St. George's, he said, "I frequently preached twice a day, at 5 o'clock in the morning and the evening, and was not uncommon for me to preach from four to five times a day. I established prayer meetings; I raised a society for forty-two members. I saw the necessity of erecting a place of worship for colored people."[43] The numeric congregational growth and additional services were praised by Methodists, but the desire to have a stand-alone church for people of color was strongly opposed by both white and black communities.[44] One of the reasons Allen and others wanted to have their own church was because St. George's started asking people of color to sit in the balcony and forbade them to sit in the pews any longer. Absalom Jones, a member of Allen's congregation, and who was later instrumental with Allen in forming the Free African Society, refused to move out of the pews. Unfortunately, this culminated in two white members physically removing Jones during the prayer, which led to other black members walking out in protest.[45] This incident and others spurred Allen and Jones on their quest for an independent black church. They started to raise money and cast a vision for a new building but came against opposition from an elder of St. George's by the name of George McClaskey:

> "If you don't stop raising money for a new church, you and your friends will be turned out of the Methodist meeting," McClaskey threatened, glaring at Allen and Jones. "Have we violated any rules of discipline by raising

42. Ryun et al., *Heroes Among Us*, 101.
43. Ibid., 102.
44. Ibid.
45. Thomas, "Richard Allen, Church-Planting Hero."

money?" Allen asked, looking at Jones, perplexed by McClaskey's words. "I have been charged by the Methodist Conference to order you to stop. If you don't, you will be publicly read out of the meeting," McClaskey replied. "We are willing to abide by the discipline of the Methodist church," Allen said. "If you will show us where we have violated any law of discipline of the church, we will submit. But if there is no rule violated, we will continue on." McClaskey was growing irritated. "We will read you and all of your friends out!" "If you turn us out contrary to the rule of discipline, we will seek redress," Allen shot back. "We were dragged off our knees at St. George's, treated worse than heathens! We will continue on, with the Lord as our helper!" "You are not Methodists!" McClaskey retorted before leaving.[46]

Though Allen wanted to stay very much a part of the Methodist Episcopal Church under which he was saved, he had trouble denying the need for an independent black church given the way God was using him in the fruitfulness of his ministry. As the fundraising was underway, more and more folks approached Allen about opening their own Methodist Church. In less than one year, Allen's congregation outgrew the building and had to expand it. In 1794, Francis Asbury preached the dedication service for the newly formed Bethel Church. Unfortunately, McClaskey attended the service and made a scene about Bethel Church having to be incorporated under the Methodist Conference. Allen obliged to the request but did not know he was signing the church's property rights over to the Methodist Conference's white members. Allen realized this after ten years had gone by when the Methodist Conference tried to appoint elder James White to Bethel Church and seize control of all the church's affairs.[47] The legal battles went back and forth as the Methodist Conference still technically owned the property and forced Allen to buy it off the auction block some fifteen years later. The Pennsylvania Supreme Court helped Allen and Bethel Church own their own property by ruling in their

46. Ryun et al., *Heroes Among Us*, 103.
47. Ibid., 106.

favor. These racial tensions and the poor treatment of black Methodists culminated in April 1816 with the formation of the first independent black denomination in America, the African Methodist Episcopal Church, and the fifteen ministers gathered together, laid hands on Allen, and elected him their first bishop.[48]

Though Allen founded Bethel Church and the AME denomination and planted numerous congregations, he was a humble servant in a bi-vocational role. Bethel Church agreed to pay Allen $500 a year for his salary support as pastor. Allen received a total of $800 of salary over thirty-five years! Despite having a low source of salary from the church Allen's business ventures helped him out. At the time of his death, Allen's estate included numerous rental properties and assets of an estimated value between $30,000 and $40,000, which in 1831 was an incredible amount of money.[49]

Because of Richard Allen's sacrifices in the early years of the AME movement, the denomination now has 7,000 congregations, with nearly 4,000 pastors, 2,510,000 in membership spanning over thirty countries and four different continents.[50] In 2012, the AME churched entered a "Pan-Methodist Celebration," an agreement of full communion and racial reconciliation with the United Methodist Church and its sister African denominations, such as African Methodist Episcopal Zion, African Union Methodist Protestant, Christian Methodist Episcopal, and Union American Methodist Episcopal. This is a direct fulfillment for what Richard Allen desperately wanted nearly two hundred years ago.[51]

---

48. Ibid., 109.

49. Thomas, "Richard Allen, Church-Planting Hero."

50. WCC, "African Methodist Episcopal Church," http://www.oikoumene.org/en/member-churches/african-methodist-episcopal-church.

51. Bloom, "Pan-Methodists Celebrate Together."

6

A Theology of Work for the Church

BI-VOCATIONAL MINISTRY MUST BE rooted in a sound theology of work. However, defining what work is can become problematic because there are many differing opinions. Because of this, I have selected some of the best definitions that are well-suited for theological conversation. Scholar David Jensen says of work, "[The] topic—human labor—is rather foreign to most systematic theologies. Not often have the codifiers of Christian doctrine explored the topic of work as an explicitly theological theme."[1] It is alarming that Jensen makes the claim that theologians have not addressed the theology of work in great detail, especially when the Bible has numerous scriptures cited about work. If the modern scholars of the church have become silent about the theology of work over time, then it becomes difficult for the church to have an understanding of the importance of bi-vocational ministry. The theology of work must come to the forefront of the church in the twenty-first century as mainline denominations are declining and facing extinction. Jensen summaries his theology of work as it pertains to Scripture by arguing,

> Biblical narratives overflow with work. Between the opening lines of Genesis, which portray God as a worker, and the closing chapter of Revelation, with a vision of new creation, God labors. One of the distinguishing

1. Jensen, *Responsive Labor*, x.

characteristics of biblical faith is that God does not sit enthroned in heaven removed from work, willing things into existence by divine fiat. Unlike the gods of the Greco-Roman mythologies, who absolve themselves of work [or make work a punishment for troublesome persons, e.g., Sisyphus] dining on nectar and ambrosia in heavenly rest and contemplation—the biblical God works.[2]

Jensen stresses how God is a working God who is not far off and aloof but a participatory God who is the creator and sustainer of the universe continually at work. Unfortunately, as New Testament scholar Ben Witherington points out, Jensen does not emphasize how humanity is to participate in collaboration with God when it comes to work.[3] Theologian Frederick Buechner defines works as "the place where your deep gladness meets the world's deep need."[4] Buechner's definition brings into account more emphasis on personal fulfillment; however, it begs the argument, as Witherington suggests, that not all activities a Christian participates in bring glory to God or edify others, like the business of war in light of Jesus's Sermon on the Mount.[5]

Theologian Miroslav Volf suggests, "Work is honest, purposeful, and methodologically specified social activity whose primary goal is the creation of products or states of affairs that can satisfy the needs of working individuals or their co-creatures, or (if primarily an end in itself) activity that is necessary in order for acting individuals to satisfy their needs apart from the need for the activity itself."[6] Again, the problem with Volf's definition is similar to Jensen's because it suggests work is a means to an end in order to gratify humanity's needs.[7] However, Volf touches on the theology of work in light of the eschatological reality Christian's live on by stating, "Christian life is life in the Spirit of the new creation or it

2. Ibid., 22.
3. Witherington, *Work*, 38.
4. Buechner, *Wishful Thinking*, 119.
5. Witherington, *Work*, 59.
6. Volf, *Work in the Spirit*, 10-11.
7. Witherington, *Work*, 60.

is not Christian life at all. And the Spirit of God should determine the whole life, spiritual as well as secular, of a Christian. Christian work must, therefore, be done under the inspiration of the Spirit and in the light of the coming new creation."[8] Therefore, work is not something that pertains to the old creation but the anticipation of a new creation when the kingdom of God comes to its fullness on earth as lived on in the Lord's Prayer when Christians pray, "Thy Kingdom come, Thy will be done on earth as it is in heaven." Jesus himself speaks about work in an eschatological framework in John 9:4 when he says, "We must work the works of him who sent me while it is day; night is coming, when no one can work." Witherington gives his definition of work with this eschatological reality in mind when he asserts that work is "any necessary and meaningful task that God calls and gifts a person to do and which can be undertaken to the glory of God and for the edification and aid of human beings, being inspired by the Spirit and foreshadowing the realities of the new creation."[9] Work was God's intention from the beginning of creation and does not cease to exist with the coming eschaton. Witherington's definition of work rocks the American understanding of work being for a certain duration of the day and season of life, like a someone working a nine-to-five job and simply looking forward to retirement. Work is a characteristic humanity must be as ingrained with as being created in the image of God.[10] An example of this is the work of monks following the Benedictine Rule at Western Priory. These monks engage in constant work and prayer by making cheeses and maple syrup to sell. They view their work and prayer together as an act of worship to God.[11] This is reminiscent of Brother Lawrence, the seventeenth-century monk from France who wrote *Practicing the Presence of God*. While working in the Discalced Carmelite monastery, he was assigned the task of kitchen duty where he cooked, cleaned, and managed the tedious chores of the monastery. Brother Lawrence

8. Volf, *Work in the Spirit*, 79.
9. Witherington, *Work*, 91.
10. Ibid., 92.
11. Ibid., 155.

did not get down on himself for these chores but learned to do them to the glory of God, as he said,

> Men invent means and methods of coming at God's love, they learn rules and set up devices to remind them of that love, and it seems like a world of trouble to bring oneself into the consciousness of God's presence. Yet it might be so simple. Is it not quicker and easier just to do our common business wholly for the love of him?[12]

Brother Lawrence had a theology of work and how it related to God's love. He did not consider "common business" as mundane work but an avenue in experiencing God's love and sharing it with the world. Brother Lawrence's writing went on to impact the like of John Wesley and A. W. Tozer to name a few.[13]

Work, when a Christian does it, no matter if it be as a custodian, chef, doctor, lawyer, or even pastor, is ministry because of the doctrine that Reformer Martin Luther emphasized, *The Priesthood of All Believers*. All Christians must participate in ministry, and a theology of work can be connected to vocation. The upper echelon of Roman society did not appreciate work that they viewed as minimal and which required one's hands to get dirty. And yet for Jews, like Jesus who was a carpenter and Paul who was a leatherworker, they did not see a distinction.[14]

---

12. "Brother Lawrence."
13. Ibid.
14. Witherington, *Work*, 387.

7

A Bi-vocational Prognosis

MY PROPOSED TREATMENT HYPOTHESIS is designed to show how Embrace Church in Lexington, Kentucky, can be a case study within mainline denominationalism as a seedbed for training missional leaders through bi-vocational and incarnational missionary methods. One of the overall purposes of this project is to develop a new model for a ministerial order that can be an example for the UMC. The current roles of elders are no longer viable in the changing context of the United States. Current approaches to itinerancy and finances are the primary factors detrimental to this new proposed approach. This new model would allow for UMC ministry to continue with fewer financial obligations and more flexibility.

Embrace Church is one congregation with four different communities in an urban context. The congregations are the Gathering, Epworth, the Downtown Campus, and a missional community in Georgetown, Kentucky. The Gathering and the Epworth congregations both meet at the 1015 North Limestone location. The Epworth congregation meets on Sunday mornings and the Gathering congregation meets on Monday evenings and includes a sit down meal, service and food pantry. The downtown congregation meets on Sunday mornings in a historic movie theater on Main Street called Kentucky Theatre. The Georgetown Missional Community meets on Sunday evenings and rotates between bible study in homes, serving together at local ministries that work with the homeless, and gathering for a larger worship celebration in a coffee shop setting. Each setting is unique and designed to reach different populations.

As a chartered UMC congregation, the UMC has placed financial restraints on Embrace Church, and these restraints have become amplified to the point that the church currently cannot financially support its operations. For many suburban and well-established churches, as they grow in attendees, their income and budgets also grow. However, when urban churches similar to Embrace Church see numerical growth, they also increase their expenses but not their expected revenue. This leaves little to no money for essential staff and ministry. This problematic scenario has called for the Embrace Church staff and membership to become better stewards with their resources and to find ways to do ministry inexpensively.

EXPECTED RESULTS

Through a team approach, the Embrace Church pastoral staff under my direction expects that the three communities that make up the church will be vital. Vitality will be measured in areas such as attendance, baptism, and professions of faith. Embrace Church will be measured against similar size congregations within the UMC in Lexington, Kentucky, to have an applicable sample pool. We seek to do this by keeping costs down and by keeping more money flowing into the ministry. The pastoral team will meet weekly to discuss accountability, support, sermon planning, and fellowship. Figure 4 shows all the specific summaries of data.

FIGURE 4.

Summary of Bi-vocational Ministry

Pastors	Roles	Measures	Outcomes
Rosario Picardo	Lead Pastor	Professions of Faiths	Sense of Calling
Chuck Gutenson	Downtown Pastor	Baptisms	Community
Bryan Langlands	Georgetown Pastor	Attendance	Blessing
Joshua Wynn	Gathering Pastor	Passion	
Justin Barringer	Outreach Pastor		

The research is examining the effectiveness of allowing flexibility to make a missional order that allows and even promotes ministers in the UMC to be bi-vocational. The pastors of Embrace Church provided themselves for an extensive time period to measure how all five of them held other ways of earning income from occupations besides being ministers so that the church would have more finances to devote to ministry. The research looked to discover how ministers could devote themselves to the workforce while leading vital congregations. The measures of effectiveness are overall worship attendance which can be defined as the number of persons who attend a given service, professions of faith which give record to people who accept Christ, and baptism which shows people who are initiated into the church. The measures all equate to vitality, which exhibits how Embrace Church is thriving at reaching people while practicing stewardship by having a smaller budget than all the churches within the UMC in Lexington, Kentucky, therefore, proving how bi-vocational ministry can be a viable option.

RESEARCH METHODS

A qualitative methodology research approach will be heavily used, which will allow for a case study of the five Embrace Church pastoral staff. A qualitative case study will be conducted through interviews with individuals and colleagues at Embrace Church, who are bi-vocational pastors and urban missionaries. This case study will be combined with narrative research; the narrative research will consist of obtaining information about the views and values of the case study participants of Embrace Church. This research seeks to measure the overall vitality of missional leaders through a complex of growth metrics that will be compared to the denominational average in a given district.[1]

I will be a researcher and participant in the study. I and the other case study participants will meet, pray, plan ministry activities, and support one another. The five participants will keep track of their attendance, professions of faith, and baptisms at Embrace Church. The interpretation of the data will help give clarity as to the effectiveness of the proposed missional model in comparison to the denomination averages.

PROJECT DESIGN

The project design began as five of the pastors at Embrace Church have voluntarily decided to become bi-vocational ministers. This project will follow their personal journeys as they seek to balance church, work, and family life. The settings are the four communities under Embrace Church that all have a different context from each other. On a weekly basis, the pastors will meet for two hours for a time of prayer, accountability, vision, and long-range planning.

1. Creswell, *Research Design*, 130-31.

Each pastor overseeing a specific community of Embrace Church will have to report their numbers in terms of weekly attendance, professions of faith, and baptisms.

DATA-ANALYSIS PROCESS

As the researcher engages a majority of their research in regards to qualitative data regarding the bi-vocational pastors, it will become particularly crucial how to analyze the data. The main data that will be analyzed when it comes to the pastors of Embrace Church is narrative data. Narrative data comes in many forms, but for this research, it will come in interview style and through the support group as the pastors meet together on a weekly basis.[2]

In addition to qualitative data, there will also be quantitative statistics added in the mix. Embrace Church will be compared to the UMC churches of similar attendance in the city of Lexington to show the effectiveness of a bi-vocational model by measuring Embrace's rank in number of baptisms and professions of faith while keeping a lean budget and showing financial stewardship.

VALIDITY

The goal of the qualitative research is to prove this study to be true and certain in regards to its findings.[3] The method used to prove this validity is triangulation. This will require recording data, conducting interviews, and comparisons of a sample pool of churches.

CREDIBILITY

The participants in this study are bi-vocational ministers. Rosario Picardo and Bryan Langlands are ordained elders given special permission to participate in being able to work a secondary job. Rosario is the lead pastor of Embrace Church, which is one

2. Ibid., 13.
3. Ibid., 149.

congregation, made up of four communities. Chuck Gutenson is a licensed local pastor in the UMC, and Joshua Wynn and Justin Barringer are staff people who also hold jobs and raise financial support. None of these pastors are paid full-time by the church but instead receive income from multiple streams.[4]

The participants were encouraged to work as much as they could, not only at Embrace Church, but also at their other places of employment. The participants happen to all be males because the one female pastor on staff is actually a full-time employee of Embrace Church.

TRANSFERABILITY

At the outset of the research, there were some assumptions made by the researcher. One was that mainline denominations such as the UMC are declining numerically in categories that will change their future as they know it. One assumed change is that there will not be as many full-time ordained elders because the cost will make it difficult for the local church to afford to pay them. Therefore, bi-vocational ministry will become the norm in the UMC in years to come as they decline. Another assumption was that bi-vocational pastors who are ministering at a church could be an effective witness in the world by showing parishioners and unchurched people that ministry is a labor of love. The third assumption was the stereotype that bi-vocational pastors may not be as effective at leading vital congregations as full-time ministers who can make more money and devote all of their work hours to the local church.

TRIANGULATION

The type of triangulation that will be used for this research project is theory triangulation. Typically, theory triangulation involves professionals outside the field, but this is not necessarily mandatory

---

4. Ibid., 192.

to show effectiveness, if the individuals are in different positions. Since the individuals in this study hold different titles and positions, the expectation is that they will draw the same conclusion thus providing validity to the research. The research is further validated as data is compiled from the four different communities under Embrace Church in regards to attendance, increased professions of faith, and increased baptisms, while keeping budget cost lower, while being compared to sample churches of similar attendance in the same setting which is the UM denomination in the city of Lexington, Kentucky. After the data is compiled, it will be shared with each individual to triangulate the information to see how they feel about it and what conclusions they draw from it.

DEPENDABILITY

In regards to research, it becomes nearly impossible to control the environment and context for which the study takes place. There are many variables that can change, especially when it comes to leadership in any given local church whether it is personal, sickness, or family circumstances. It is important for the researcher to keep up to date on individuals who are involved in this bi-vocational case study to monitor for any changes that could affect the research.

CONFIRMABILITY

The researcher believes that the results of the qualitative study research will be confirmed by the individuals who are participating in it. The researcher will keep track of the positive and negative experiences that the bi-vocational pastors have throughout the case study. Once the study is complete then a data audit will reveal the effectiveness of the overall project.

PROJECT TIMELINE

2012

June 4	Bi-vocational pastor, Chuck Gutenson comes on staff
September 3	Lead Pastor, Rosario Picardo becomes bi-vocational
October 11	Bi-vocational elder, Bryan Langlands begins Georgetown Missional Community

2013

January 7	Urban Missionary, Josh Wynn becomes pastoral leader of the Gathering
April 7	Chuck Gutenson becomes downtown campus pastor
May 20	Urban Missionary, Justin Barringer joins staff
June-Dec	Monthly incubator 8-hour meetings
June-Dec	Interviews will be conducted

BI-VOCATIONAL PASTOR INTERVIEW QUESTIONS

John W. Creswell states that in qualitative interviews the researcher conducts face-to-face, telephone, or focus group interviews, and each group should contain six to eight interviewees. A few unstructured and open-ended questions should be asked with the intent to elicit views and opinions.[5] The following four open-ended questions will be asked in this project:

- Why have you decided to come on staff at Embrace Church as a bi-vocational pastor?

---

5. Ibid., 181.

- How has making this decision impacted your life, your family, and Embrace Church?
- What type of growth have you seen as a result of being on staff at Embrace Church?
- What challenges have you faced as a bi-vocational pastor?

A definition of terms is necessary to define what exactly is a bi-vocational pastor. For this study, a bi-vocational pastor is one who works a job(s) outside of Embrace Church and receives little or no financial salary from the church or who may raise a financial support from benefactors outside of Embrace Church's context. In the course of the interviews for the qualitative analysis there were four common patterns involving the bi-vocational pastors of Embrace Church as seen in figure 5.

FIGURE 5.

Common Patterns

Catergorical Pattern	Definition
Sense of Calling	They are each on staff as bi-vocational because they feel that God has called them to do ministry in this way.
Community	There is a sense that community (other staff and other church people) has been the greatest thing for accountability in these pastors' lives. Also, community plays a big role in each of the success stories that they share (the person who is lonely or outcast is now surrounded and a part of the community).

Catergorical Pattern	Definition
Blessing	Each pastor expressed that being on staff has been an overall blessing in spite of difficulties with finances, lack of time, etc. You get a sense that each would make the same decision to be a bi-vocational pastor if given the opportunity to make the choice again.

SENSE OF CALLING

The common pattern of calling is an important theme in this particular study, throughout the Scriptural characters selected with Paul, Nehemiah, and Amos, and historically with the early Methodist Circuit Riders. The bi-vocational pastors of Embrace Church would not engage in the work they do without feeling a compelling call by God. John Wesley, the founder of Methodism recognized two facets of calling to ministry. The first is an *inner call*, which is confirmed through the gifts and graces for ministry that one is given. It is the Holy Spirit stirring in an individual as God speaks to their heart much like the Prophet Jeremiah who had a compelling message to share and said that he needed to share it because "it was like fire shut up in his bones." A second necessary facet is the *outward call*, which comes from outside an individual through the church. People in the community of faith affirm a person in their giftings and encourage them to pursue and exercise the giftings in the community.[6]

Embrace Church's bi-vocational ministers are a blend of how both the work of the clergy and laity can work in a harmonious way. Wesley's understanding of ministry influenced the rest of the Wesleyan tradition by the belief that the ordained ministry was

---

6. Campbell, *Yoke of Obedience*, 53.

apart from a preaching ministry, which Wesley believed anybody could pursue. Early Methodism expected their laity and preachers to adhere to an exemplary life with works of piety and spiritual disciplines. Wesley did not come up with Methodism to be a separate faction but to be a renewal group of sorts remaining under the larger umbrella of the Church of England. Wesley deeply cared for the spiritual well-being of all under the care of early Methodism. Wesley's concern was over the needs for Methodists to receive the sacraments. Because of this need for pastoral care, Wesley was persuaded to ordain Francis Asbury and Thomas Coke as ministers in order for them to administer the sacraments.[7]

Ultimately, Wesley's call for renewal within the Church of England burdened his heart for outreach in his context. As Methodism grew and expanded to the United States, Wesley knew the context was going to change and the approach was going to as well. It was because of this that he ordained Asbury and Coke. Likewise, many of the early circuit riders traveled a great distance because of the calling they felt to reach new people for the gospel. Early Methodism was a church planting movement to its core, and Embrace Church is living within that tradition as God is raising up bi-vocational ministers to carry out the task.

The Gathering pastor of Embrace Church, Joshua Wynn, shares the following about calling:

> First, I felt God calling me to be on staff at Embrace in an Urban Missionary position, specifically as the pastor of The Gathering. Second, along with that calling, God had given me a love for the people and the vision of Embrace. In a lot of ways, I was that hurt, broken person that we talk about, and God has definitely done some amazing work in my own life.[8]

Outreach pastor of Embrace Church, Justin Barringer, mentioned calling as a top reason as to why he decided to be a bi-vocational minister at Embrace Church. Barringer said:

---

7. Ibid.

8. Wynn, "Bi-vocational Pastor Interview Questions."

> My wife and I both felt that [Embrace Church] is where we were called. If it's the place you are called, you should go, regardless of whether or not you have all the plans worked out. I think part of the reason we discerned that this is the place we are called is that the stuff we saw and still see there is very kingdom-oriented. Also, we felt a more general call in terms of living in a neighborhood where there is poverty.[9]

The Georgetown Missional pastor of Embrace Church, Bryan Langlands, affirmed the reason he wanted to join Embrace's staff was a call to be a part of a new church start. Langlands explained,

> I felt like it was a calling from the Lord to be involved in a church plant, to a new church start, a new faith community. That opportunity presented itself, and I had some conversations with you. I think part of it was a conversation that we had a few years ago about that vision God had given you about different outposts of Embrace in different parts of Lexington and maybe up in Georgetown. We started talking about maybe calling it Embrace-Georgetown or something like that to make that connection with the church real visible and apparent. You know, just a prompting of the Lord to do that. I think it is a phase of apostolic ministry, of being sent out, and starting new things, that the Lord has called me into.[10]

The interesting part of the bi-vocational ministers of Embrace Church is that the lead pastor, Rosario Picardo, and Georgetown Missional pastor, Bryan Langlands, are the only ordained elders. Chuck Gutenson is a part-time local pastor and Joshua Wynn and Justin Barringer are staff members. Picardo believes that part of his ordained ministry is to start a renewal movement within the UMC. When a Methodist minister is admitted into full connection, they make a covenant, which is something that is not self-seeking but instead sacrificial. This is a reminder of John Wesley's Covenant

---

9. Barringer, "Bi-vocational Pastor Interview Questions."
10. Langlands, "Bi-vocational Pastor Interview Questions."

Service when it is said, "We take upon ourselves with joy the yoke of obedience . . . We are no longer our own but thine."[11]

COMMUNITY

The segment of calling that is often neglected is that communal aspect of it. Embrace Church's bi-vocational pastors have a sense of being called into community together for mutual accountability. This has been involved in meeting weekly for eight to ten hours a month through prayer, scripture reading, accountability, and encouragement. All the pastors surveyed said there is a strong sense that community (with other staff and other church people) has been the greatest thing for accountability in these pastors' lives. Also, community plays a big role in each of the success stories that they share (the person who is lonely or outcast is now surrounded and a part of the community).

In terms of accountability there would be "missional accountability" items that each staff member would be assigned to do. The researcher would define missional accountability as a task or duty that would be either relational or administrative that needed to be accomplished to further the mission of Embrace Church. In addition to the missional accountability items, a reminder email would be sent to all staff members.

The reality of a having a majority of staff as bi-vocational pastors is that their time is limited between the balance of family, children, finances, and working additional jobs or raising support. The missional accountability is one aid for the mission to be accomplished, and the other is a weekly productivity report. The weekly productivity report served as a source of accountability for the bi-vocational pastors and also as a way for the researcher and lead pastor, Rosario Picardo, to monitor progress. It included weekly accomplishments, a list of ongoing projects, contacts made in the week, questions or concerns, and prayer requests.

---

11. Campbell, *Yoke of Obedience*, 18.

The community component that the bi-vocational pastors experienced in their time together was patterned after the Wesleyan band meetings. The accountability factor was seen more clearly in bands because the band meetings were much smaller, consisting of about six to eight members with leadership selected from within the group. This can be seen in Wesley's own life where intimate interaction was played out in the Holy Club, in Georgia with the Sunday afternoon gatherings, the Fetter Lane Society, and then the band meetings of early Methodism. The idea of the band meeting was the distinguishing factor between the ministries of Wesley and George Whitefield. Even though Whitefield was considered to be a more dynamic preacher than Wesley, his efforts did not provide a long lasting discipleship. Wesley believed that the most effective way to follow up his field preaching was by establishing discipleship opportunities such as the bands. The band meeting was said to be Wesley's favorite meeting, though the class meeting provided the instructional mode for early Methodists. The original mode of Methodism was the band meeting, and it was from Wesley's quest to perfect it that others sprang forth.[12] The band meeting was elevated to the middle level in the system while the rise of the class meeting in 1742 became the entry group to supplant the band.[13] The band meeting was not mandatory of Methodism but was strongly encouraged by the societies and class meetings.[14]

The bands were organized by separating men from women, married and singles, kids and adults. The basis of the *Rules of the Bands* was on James 5:16, "Confess your faults to another, and pray for one another that you may be healed."[15] Participants were to meet once a week, come punctually at the hour appointed, begin with singing or prayer, and speak the true state of their souls: sharing any faults and temptations since the last meeting, and if they had victory over it, explaining how they resisted it.[16] A leader was

---

12. Ibid., 112.
13. Henderson, *John Wesley's Class Meeting*, 115.
14. Ibid., 116.
15. KJV.
16. Wesley, "Plain Account," 272.

to speak their state first and then go around the room; however, if a person did not share much the leader would ask them more pointed questions.[17] Bands aided participants in striving toward sanctification by providing a safe environment where sins and temptations could be shared without reserve but in all honesty. The intense confessional aspect of the band meetings made them unique from the class meeting and societies, and a smaller group made it more attractive to divulge a person's shadow side. This allowed band members to become close knit groups because they discovered that sharing struggles, advice, and prayer helped in the bonding process.[18]

A return to early Methodism involves commitment to areas of discipline that would help shed light on today's concerns for the small group movement. A step in the right direction for today's small groups would be to make a return to Wesley's day where early Methodists adhered to a set of practices known as the *General Rules of the United Societies*, which helped them in maintaining their relationship with God and their neighbor. The three rules of discipline asked Christians to serve God in the following ways:

> 1. By doing no harm, by avoiding evil in every kind . . .
> 2. By doing good, by being in every kind merciful after their power, as they have opportunity doing good of every possible sort . . . to all . . . : to their bodies . . . ; to their souls . . . 3. By attending all the ordinances of God. Such are: the public worship of God; the ministry of the word, either read or expounded; the Supper of the Lord; family and private prayer; searching the Scriptures; and fasting or abstinence.[19]

Though each rule has specific rules under each one, they must be viewed in a holistic manner. The first rule emphasizes how one's actions must reflect reverence to both God and neighbor.[20] The second rule focuses on Christian formation and evangelism

17. Henderson, *John Wesley's Class Meeting*, 118.
18. Knight, *Eight Life-Enriching Practices*, 82.
19. Wesley, "Plain Account," Nature, Design, and General Rules, 270.
20. Wesley, "Plain Account," Directions Given to the Band-Societies, 273.

involving the soul, social concerns having to do with the physical body which are "works of mercy."[21] The "works of piety" encompassed in the third rule makes mention of our love for God through the overlapping of the means of grace.[22]

To become "disciplined" in the sense of the word for early Methodists was to leave behind their former pre-Christian lives. It was to turn away from activities that would place a wedge between one's relationship with God and with their neighbor. Such activities would include profanity, quarreling, gossiping, lying, greed, and fulfilling selfish desires. The behavior, which was encouraged of early Methodist, was to take care of the poor and down trodden of society, to care for the social outcasts by encouraging others through the gospel to live a life of holiness. This type of behavior of early Methodists was not a "social club" mentality where group meetings were only about the participants. Instead meetings were intended to help the participant grow deeper spiritually by living an inward and outward Christian life that interacted with the society in which they lived.[23]

The gathering pastor at Embrace Church, Joshua Wynn, attributes his success for ministry as a bi-vocational pastor because of staff meeting accountability. In Joshua's own words he says,

> Community is key for accountability. So, my time spent with Chuck on a weekly basis and my time spent with everyone else at the staff meetings help me stay accountable. The progress reports help me stay accountable because I can look through and see what I have done and what I haven't. And having someone help you is very beneficial and holds you accountable. When you feel that you are doing it all by yourself, it's hard to stay accountable.[24]

Justin Barringer, outreach pastor of Embrace Church, says of community and accountability,

---

21. Ibid., 274.
22. Ibid.
23. Knight, *Eight Life-Enriching Practices*, 81.
24. Wynn, "Bi-vocational Pastor Interview Questions."

That's been a huge help for us. Just having community around us that encourages us, questions us, and prays for us. I feel that we could be doing a lot of good things and really easily get way off track if we didn't have the community. I don't even think that we would try, if we didn't have the community. A lot of the tasks are not me doing a task; it's us doing a task. So, naturally, since we are doing it in community, even if one person is heading it up, accountability is built in.[25]

BLESSING

In the case study research of the bi-vocational pastors of Embrace Church a third significant pattern noted was that of blessing. Each pastor expressed that being on staff has been an overall blessing in spite of difficulties with finances and lack of time. You get a sense that each would make the same decision to be a bi-vocational pastor if given the opportunity to make the choice again. The comments below are in response to the question "What challenges have you faced as a bi-vocational pastor?" at Embrace Church in particular. Their responses are below:

> Oh, the usual too little money for all we want to do, difficult folks who function passive aggressively, a great weakness in churches, I think. Processes can be slow and unwieldy. (Chuck Gutenson)

> Well, it's been tough, but for most of my marriage we haven't been in great financial standing since we were in China and I was a student for most of my marriage. But for me I feel like I'm doing the stuff that I'm supposed to be doing for the most part, so that's been very good. I think it's been difficult because last month we weren't able to meet our budget. (Justin Barringer)

> Fundraising has been a challenge, obviously, but you know God has helped me with that. I think the hardest

25. Barringer, "Bi-vocational Pastor Interview Questions."

challenge for me is with the people I serve, that I really do life with day in and day out, there is a lot of neediness and a lot of brokenness. And there is a lot of hurt and a lot of pain. On Monday nights, as soon as I walk out of my office, there is someone waiting to tell me another heartbreaking story. And so the challenge for me is as a pastor to be that shepherd but . . . [to] know when enough is enough, to separate yourself so that it doesn't begin to hurt you, if that makes sense. That is one of the biggest challenges that I have faced. There are days where you feel drained because the issues that people are facing are so big, and sometimes you feel like you can do so little, and it makes you question things like is love really enough sometimes . . . Learning to set boundaries and not always pick up the phone when someone is out of food. And then also, another challenge is discernment and one of the things you and me have talked about is that there are people who will waste your time or want to take up all your time. And I have a lot of that with some of the people I am in relationship with. Sometimes they will want to talk to me about the same thing over and over again for two to three hours at a time. Sometimes that can be distracting when there is someone else who really, really is hurting or in really major need or needs to be comforted or needs to be helped. So discernment is a challenge. Let's see. What else are challenges? I think sometimes you have challenges with just working with a team. Although it is a great community, there are different ideas and different visions. God has created us differently and made us to think differently, or perhaps our backgrounds, where we have come from, make us think in different ways. Sometimes there are conflicts or different feelings that go along with that. That can always be a challenge, but at the same time, it can be a huge blessing. There were times where I didn't really think holistically about something, and maybe LeTicia or you have said something that has made me think differently about something. So while it is a challenge, iron sharpens iron, right? Challenges should be considered places to grow rather than negative things. (Joshua Wynn)

It's been a blessing overall, but it has been a challenge at times. We have three young children, so time is one of our most precious commodities. There have been moments and weeks where the responsibilities of being in leadership with this missional community have felt like a sacrifice just because we are time-pinched. Overall, we are trying. My wife Amanda is an ordained pastor as well, and our primary way of doing things is that we try not to compartmentalize because we see our fundamental ministry as our family ministry. Together as a family, we are living our mission together. Sometimes that means as a family we are at momma's church doing stuff. Sometimes that means we're at daddy's church doing stuff. Sometimes that means we are hosting college students in our home. The primary thing is our family trying to be on mission together as a family. My daughters . . . I've been talking to them about what it means to be missionaries for Jesus in their schools and playgrounds. And so, really it's been one more opportunity to be a family on mission together through the things that the Movement has been doing. Realistically, when we have had our public worship gatherings, because we have had them Sunday nights, my family hasn't always been able to be involved. Sometimes, my wife has Sunday night meetings at her church. We have a one-year-old, so having her there while I'm also trying to lead can be difficult. If my wife can't be there, then that's pretty much challenging. I've asked other people to help out with that but overall, it's been a blessing. (Bryan Langlands)

FINANCIAL IMPACT OF BI-VOCATIONAL MINISTRY

The researcher and participant in the study, Rosario Picardo, is an ordained elder in the UMC. As well as being a lead pastor of Embrace Church, Picardo also works for the Lexington District of the UMC as a New Church Development Coordinator and is the founder of Picardo Coaching LLC. Picardo is one of the lowest paid ordained elders in the Kentucky Annual Conference (KAC) by choice because of missional reasons. Picardo's total compensation package is roughly around $48,000. Chuck Gutenson is a part-time local pastor with Embrace Church and receives $12,000 annually for overseeing the downtown community. Joshua Wynn is the Gathering pastor who receives no compensation from Embrace Church. Wynn raises support as an urban missionary along with doing odd jobs such as home repairs and lawn care. Justin Barringer, outreach pastor of Embrace Church, receives no compensation from the church. Barringer also works at a nonprofit, the Lexington Rescue Mission. Bryan Langlands, pastor of Georgetown Missional Community, receives no compensation from the church. Langlands is a full-time campus minister with Georgetown College. The total budgetary impact for Embrace Church due these five bi-vocational pastors is $60,000. This is saving Embrace Church thousands of dollars knowing that the minimum compensation package for ordained elders in the KAC is $71,031 (as seen in figure 6) and the average compensation package for ordained elders is $101,780 for one minister (as seen in figure 7).

FIGURE 6.

The Minimum Compensation Package for Ordained Elders in Kentucky

Package Category	Cost
Base Salary	$34,195
Parsonage or Housing Allowance	$12,000
Utilities and other allowances	$4,000
Retirement and life insurance contributions	$7,576
Health Insurance Provided	$13,260

Total package: $71,031

FIGURE 7.

2013 Average Compensation for Ordained Elders in Kentucky

Package Category	Cost
Base Salary	$61,055
Parsonage or Housing Allowance	$12,000** **(This is minimum allowed—the average wasn't listed)
Utilities and other allowances	$4,000
Retirement and life insurance contributions	$11,981
Health Insurance Provided	$12,744

Total package: $101,780 (assuming minimum-level housing and utilities allowance)

Embrace Church has found a creative way to maintain its attendance, entrepreneurial spirit, and meet the needs of the congregations with these bi-vocational pastors. Embrace is paving a future reality for most UMC churches where the money is running out. It is not sustainable for churches to be able to afford ordained elders. Other denominations and faith traditions have promoted bi-vocational ministry for this very reason.

RESULTS OF BI-VOCATIONAL MINISTRY

As indicated prior to this, the success of the project was going to be dependent on the outcomes Embrace Church was going to measure. These included worship attendance, professions of faith, and baptisms. Embrace Church's 2012 statistics were taken and compared to the 2013 statistics to see how they measured with their bi-vocational leaders in place with the diverse communities as seen in figure 8.

FIGURE 8.

2012 Embrace Church Statistics Compared to 2013 Statistics[26]

	Attendance	Professions of Faith	Baptisms
2012	265	40	10
2013	300	72	13
% Growth	13.2%	80%	30%

These statistics are important because they confirm that a healthy bi-vocational model for ministry is a viable option for churches that are seeking a more cost effective but high impact way of doing ministry.

---

26. These were numbers that were compiled by Embrace Church and reported to the Kentucky Annual Conference of the UMC.

8

Rethinking Church

IT HAS BEEN A central theme of this text to understand that there has been a significant decline within the UMC and in all mainline denominations. The decline has been seen through drops in worship attendance, membership, professions of faith, and baptisms, as well as through church closures. All the people-based categories have decreased, but the financial expenses have increased over the past forty years, especially considering inflation. The solution has been to reset the financial baseline by introducing a model for recovering a theology of bi-vocational ministry within the UMC, focusing on opportunities for planting new faith communities, and rethinking stewardship of the church's resources as a whole.

Within the UMC, the level of trust between laity and clergy could be greatly impacted in a positive way by not only modifying the appointment system with selection of clergy, but also limiting the itinerancy process. The way the UMC understands itinerancy is not what it was originally meant to be. As George Hunter explains, the church planters of early Methodism were the circuit-riding pastors who targeted territories instead of being appointed to churches.[1] Hunter recalls, "In frontier America circuit-riding pastors were not appointed to churches; they were appointed to territories. Circuit riders planted churches to reach the people in the communities, and everywhere, first generation Methodist laity

---

1. Hunter, *Recovery*, 954.

reached far more people than the preachers did."[2] Even Wesley himself makes distinctions between the different roles of people involved in ministry, which sheds some light on what is intended for itinerancy in his sermon entitled, "The Ministerial Office":

> But I do not find that ever the office of an Evangelist was the same with that of a Pastor, frequently called a Bishop. He presided over the flock, and administered the sacraments: The former assisted him, and preached the Word, either in one or more congregations. I cannot prove from any part of the New Testament, or from any author of the three first centuries, that the office of an Evangelist gave any man a right to act as a Pastor or Bishop. I believe these offices were considered as quite distinct from each other till the time of Constantine.[3]

Wesley is clear to make the distinction that traveling preachers are not pastors. The circuit riders could come every few weeks, gather crowds, and preach the Word. However, it is the role of the stationary local elders and laity to invest in the long-term growth of Methodism. The stability of local elders and laity has a direct impact on the health of a congregation. Too often, congregations split or simply decline when elders are moved prematurely due to itinerancy. According to Donald Haynes, the UMC has become so bound to itinerancy that it has obtained a reputation as "the church that moves its preachers a lot," instead of being known by its theology and Wesleyan distinctive.[4] As it is practiced now, itinerancy is a long-standing and deeply rooted tradition. For the UMC, this shift in practice is necessary, even though it would be a significant move for the denomination.

It should not come as a surprise that many church leaders may not be in favor of making these shifts in the church. Within the UMC, a major impact of making the shift from itinerant appointments to more singular appointments would mean ordained elders may no longer receive guaranteed appointments, and the

2. Ibid.
3. Wesley, "Ministerial Office."
4. Haynes, quoted by Williams, "On Message and Method."

rethinking and redistribution of resources would mean bishops, district superintendents, administrators and clergy will no longer receive a top-tier rate of pay or the excessively high cost benefits package that accompanies these positions. Across the board, church leaders will be faced with the challenges of possibly working another job while engaged in ministry as a vocation, accepting a lower rate of pay for "ministry work," redefining worship/ministry space in more modest terms, and adjusting to a major cut in spending kingdom resources on excessive commodities that have been passed off as ministry necessities.

It is evident that the church could use a serious ministry makeover. However, whether leaders actually embrace this work is a different story. Although, these changes would be transformational on many different levels and especially in the community, it is uncomfortable work that will require a lot of selflessness and sacrifice. It puts Jesus's teachings about self-denial and carrying the cross into a different perspective when we are actually challenged to be the church and do it.

The case study of Embrace Church as a bi-vocational model for ministry that engages in the work of rethinking resources shows that this paradigm shift can be effective for congregations that struggle to meet annual budget or congregations that simply want to become more fiscally responsible stewards of kingdom resources. When considering the bi-vocational component, it is important to take into account context along with the attitude of a given congregation. This model works best in settings where the individuals under consideration for leadership are called to serve in a bi-vocational role. Embrace is proud to be one of the churches engaged in the work of ministry makeover. Hopefully, it will be a catalyst for transformation within the UMC and mainline denominations across North America.

Bibliography

Anderson, Bernhard W. *The Living World of the Old Testament*. Harlow, UK: Longman, 1988.
Barringer, Justin. "Bi-vocational Pastor Interview Questions." Interview by author. Embrace Church, Lexington, Kentucky, March 2014.
Blanchard, John. "Amos." In *Major Points from the Minor Prophets*, 809-1214. Darlington, UK: Evangelical Press, 2012. Kindle edition.
Bloom, Linda. "Pan-Methodists Celebrate Together." *UMConnections* (United Methodist Church blog), May 1, 2012. http://umcconnections.org/2012/05/01/pan-methodists-celebrate-together.
The Book of Discipline of the United Methodist Church. 2008 ed. Nashville: United Methodist Publishing House, 2008.
"Brother Lawrence." *Christian Classics Ethereal Library*. http://www.ccel.org/ccel/lawrence.
Brown, Raymond. *The Message of Nehemiah: God's Servant in a Time of Change*. Leicester, UK: InterVarsity, 1998.
Bruce, F. F. *The Book of the Acts*. Grand Rapids: Eerdmans, 1988.
Buechner, Frederick. *Wishful Thinking: A Seeker's ABC*. San Francisco: HarperSanFrancisco, 1993.
Calvin, John. "Commentary on Amos, Part 16." Sion's Jewish Instruction Pages. http://www.iclnet.org/pub/resources/text/m.sion/cvams-16.htm.
Campbell, Dennis M. *The Yoke of Obedience: The Meaning of Ordination in Methodism*. Nashville: Abingdon, 1988.
Couey, J. Blake. "Amos VII 10-17 and Royal Attitudes toward Prophecy in the Ancient Near East." *Vetus Testamentum* 58 (2008) 300-14.
Creswell, John W. *Research Design: Qualitative, Quantitative, and Mixed Methods Approaches*. Los Angeles: Sage, 2009. Kindle edition.
Dorsett, Terry W. *Developing Leadership Teams in the Bivocational Church*. Bloomington, IN: CrossBooks, 2010. Kindle edition.
Fee, Gordon D. "First Word for the Disruptive-Idle: Imitate Paul (3:7-10)." In *The First and Second Letters to the Thessalonians*. Grand Rapids: Eerdmans, 2009. Kindle edition.
Fensham, F. Charles. *The Books of Ezra and Nehemiah*. Grand Rapids: Eerdmans, 1982. Kindle edition.

BIBLIOGRAPHY

Ferreiro, Alberto, and Thomas C. Oden. "Amos 7:1-17." In *The Twelve Prophets*, 109–10. Ancient Christian Commentary on Scripture, Old Testament 14. Downers Grove: InterVarsity, 2003.

Finley, Thomas John. *Joel, Amos, Obadiah: An Exegetical Commentary*. Dallas: Biblical Studies, 2003.

Giles, Terry. "A Note on the Vocation of Amos in 7:14." *Journal of Biblical Literature* 111 (1992) 690-91. http://connection.ebscohost.com/c/literary-criticism/7158903/note-vocation-amos-7-14.

Good, Kenneth R. "The Life and Times of Jacob Albright." Albright College sesquicentennial. http://www.albright.edu/150/lifeandtimes.html.

Gutenson, Charles E. "Bi-vocational Pastor Interview Questions." Interview by author. Embrace Church, Lexington, Kentucky, March 2014.

Hahn, Heather. "2011 Numbers Show U.S. Members Still Sliding." UMC.org. August 2, 2012. http://www.umc.org/news-and-media/2011-numbers-show-us-members-still-sliding.

Hays, J. Daniel, and Tremper Longman. "Overview of Amos." In *Message of the Prophets: A Survey of the Prophetic and Apocalyptic Books of the Old Testament*, 4347-57. Grand Rapids: Zondervan, 2010. Kindle edition.

Heitzenrater, Richard P. *Wesley and the People Called Methodists*. Nashville: Abingdon, 1995.

Henderson, D. Michael. *John Wesley's Class Meeting: A Model for Making Disciples*. Nappanee, IN: Evangel, 1997

Henry, Matthew. *Matthew Henry's Commentary on the Whole Bible: Complete and Unabridged in One Volume*. Peabody: Hendrickson, 1994.

Hock, Ronald F. "Paul's Tentmaking and the Problem of His Social Class." *Journal of Biblical Literature* 97 (1978) 555–64. Old Testament Abstracts, EBSCOhost.

―――. *The Social Context of Paul's Ministry: Tentmaking and Apostleship*. Philadelphia: Fortress, 1980.

Hunter, George G. *The Recovery of a Contagious Methodist Movement*. Nashville: Abingdon, 2011. Kindle edition.

Jensen, David Hadley. *Responsive Labor: A Theology of Work*. Louisville: Westminster John Knox, 2006.

Joyner, F. Belton. *United Methodist Questions, United Methodist Answers: Exploring Christian Faith*. Louisville: Westminster John Knox, 2007.

―――. *The Unofficial United Methodist Handbook for Pastors*. Nashville: Abingdon, 2007. Kindle edition.

Keller, Marie Noël. "Luke's Narration." In *Priscilla and Aquila: Paul's Coworkers in Christ Jesus*, 441-42. Collegeville: Liturgical, 2010. Kindle edition.

Kinghorn, Kenneth C. *The Heritage of American Methodism*. Strasbourg, France: Signe, 1999.

Langlands, Bryan. "Bi-vocational Pastor Interview Questions." Interview by author. Embrace Church, Lexington, Kentucky, March 2014.

Martin, Francis, and Thomas C. Oden. *Acts*. Ancient Christian Commentary on Scripture 5. Downers Grove: InterVarsity, 2006.

BIBLIOGRAPHY

McKinley, Rick. "New England Annual Conference." Telephone interview by author, March 30, 2014. McKinley is the New Church Development Director for the New England Annual Conference of the UMC.

Miller, George. *Short Description of the Effective Grace of God in the Enlightened, Protestant Preacher, Jacob Albright*. Translated and edited by James D. Nelson. http://united.edu/wp-content/uploads/2014/01/albright-english.pdf.

Montana, Sam. "What Caused the Great Recession of 2008-2009?" September 2010. https://economics-the-economy.knoji.com/what-caused-the-great-recession-of-20082009.

Nelson, John. *An Extract of John Nelson's Journal Being an Account of God's Dealing with His Soul . . . Written by Himself*. Bristol, 1767.

———. *The Lives of Early Methodist Preachers*. Edited by Thomas Jackson. Vol. 1. London: Wesleyan Conference Office, 1865.

PBS. "Richard Allen." In *Africans in America*. Part 3, *1791–1831*. http://www.pbs.org/wgbh/aia/part3/3p97.html.

Perkins, John. *With Justice for All: A Strategy for Community Development*. Ventura, CA: Regal, 2007. Kindle edition.

Rapske, Brian. *The Book of Acts and Paul in Roman Custody*. Grand Rapids: Eerdmans, 1994.

Rendle, Gilbert R. *Journey in the Wilderness: New Life for Mainline Churches*. Nashville: Abingdon, 2010. Kindle edition.

Ryun, Jim, et al. *Heroes Among Us: Deep within Each of Us Dwells the Heart of a Hero*. Shippensburg, PA: Treasure House, 2002. Kindle edition.

Shockley, Gary A. "New Church Starts Update." Statistical update on Quadrennial Goals. *Path1.org*, April 19, 2012.

Simmons, Martha J., and Frank A. Thomas. *Preaching with Sacred Fire: An Anthology of African American Sermons, 1750 to the Present*. New York: Norton, 2010. Kindle edition.

Simundson, Daniel J. Amos and Amaziah. In *Hosea, Joel, Amos, Obadiah, Jonah, Micah*, 218–23. Nashville: Abingdon, 2005.

"The Story of Boehm and Otterbein." UB.org, website of the Church of the United Brethren in Christ, USA. http://ub.org/about/boehm-otterbein.

Stuart, Douglas K. *Hosea-Jonah*. Word Biblical Commentary 31. Waco, TX: Word, 1982.

Thomas, John. "Richard Allen, Church-Planting Hero." February 7, 2012. http://newcitychurch.org/2012/02/07/richard-allen-church-planting-hero.

Throntveit, Mark A. *Ezra-Nehemiah*. Interpretation. Louisville: John Knox, 1992. Kindle edition.

Vincent, M. R. *Word Studies in the New Testament*. New York: Scribner, 1887.

Volf, Miroslav. *Work in the Spirit: Toward a Theology of Work*. New York: Oxford University Press, 1991.

Weems, Lovett H. *Focus: The Real Challenges That Face the United Methodist Church*. Nashville: Abingdon, 2012. Kindle edition.

Bibliography

Wesley, John. "The Ministerial Office." Sermon 115. http://www.umcmission.org/Find-Resources/Global-Worship-and-Spiritual-Growth/John-Wesley-Sermons/Sermon-115-The-Ministerial-Office.

———. "A Plain Account of the People Called Methodist." In *The Works of John Wesley*, edited by Rupert E. Davis, 9:253–80. Nashville: Abingdon, 1989.

———. *The Works of John Wesley*. Vol. 3. Reprint. Amazon Digital Services. Kindle edition.

Williams, Guy M. "On Message and Method." Guy M. Williams's blog. April 21, 2008. http://guymwilliams.net/2008/04/21/on-message-and-method.

Willimon, William H., and Robert L. Wilson. "Rekindling the Flame." Chap. 1. Nashville: Abingdon, 1987. Available at http://www.cmpage.org/rekindling/chapt1.html.

Witherington, Ben. *1 and 2 Thessalonians: A Socio-Rhetorical Commentary*. Grand Rapids: Eerdmans, 2006.

———. *New Testament History: A Narrative Account*. Grand Rapids: Baker Academic, 2001. Kindle edition.

———. *The Paul Quest: The Renewed Search for the Jew of Tarsus*. Downers Grove: InterVarsity, 1998. Kindle edition.

———. *Work: A Kingdom Perspective on Labor*. Grand Rapids: Eerdmans, 2011. Kindle edition.

Wood, Fred. "Clash between Amaziah and Amos (vv. 10-17)." In *Amos*, 120–21. Minor Prophets Series. Bloomington, IN: CrossBooks, 2009.

Wynn, Joshua. "Bi-vocational Pastor Interview Questions." Interview by author. Embrace Church, Lexington, Kentucky, March 2014.

Yrigoyen, Charles, and Susan E. Warrick. *Historical Dictionary of Methodism*. Lanham, MD: Scarecrow, 1996.

www.ingramcontent.com/pod-product-compliance
Lightning Source LLC
Chambersburg PA
CBHW070514090426
42735CB00012B/2772